Paying Your Way:

Improving Performance through Uptime

Paying Your Way
Improving Performance through Uptime

James V. Reyes-Picknell

Foreword by:

James K. Gowans

Conscious Group Inc. 2020

First Printing: 2020

ISBN ISBN #: 978-1-79486-723-9

Conscious Group Inc.,
92 Caplan Avenue
Barrie, ON L4N 9J2
Canada
www.consciousasset.com
info@consciousasset.com
+1 705 408 0255

Special discounts are available on quantity purchases by corporations, associations, educators, and others. For details, contact the publisher at the above listed address, email or phone number.

Dedication

To my wife Aileen.

Thank you. Without your support, encouragement and patience,
I would have never achieved this milestone.

Contents

Acknowledgements

My good friend, Len Middleton, and my wife, Aileen, have both played major roles in the production of this book. Both contributed extensive editing input and help with graphic presentation of concepts. Len is and has been my sounding board for many matters and his help in crystallizing concepts is invaluable to me. Aileen was likewise invaluable in ensuring both wording and graphics were readable and that they would make sense to the non-technical reader. Len and Aileen, without your support and help this book would not have been possible. Thank you!

Thank you for your patience and guidance, your use of the editor's red pen, your creative ideas and insistence on both precision and a bit of humor.

Aileen arranged for a wonderful graphic artist to help with our figures. I'd like to thank Michael Trapani of Incube8 Creative for his graphic contributions to this effort.

In my consulting career I've met some truly outstanding individuals. One in particular was my first boss as a consultant, and he became a close friend, John Dixon Campbell. He was the author of the first edition of "Uptime – Strategies for Excellence in Maintenance Management", and he was the partner who hired me into Coopers & Lybrand – one of the then "big five" multi-discipline consulting firms. John was my mentor as my consulting skills were being developed and much of what I do and how I manage today was learned from him. We had a practice in Physical Asset Management, yet so much of what we did was all about people, their perceptions, their passions, and their behaviors. I learned that our technical-looking discipline is really all about people and change. You've been gone since 2002 John, but you are alive in my heart and in my passion for what I do. From you I learned the value of balance in our "Uptime" approach to helping our customers improve. Thank you for continuing to be with me in spirit, if not in body.

Another mentor who had a great deal of influence in my career was John Moubray. John took the early airline industry version of Reliability Centered Maintenance and turned it into a viable commercial product using a functional approach. Once my thinking about machines changed from "things" to "functions", and from "managing failures" to "managing consequences", a whole world of possibility opened up. My application of RCM up to that point was limited by the need to dig into details about parts – it was mind-numbing. John freed me from that and imparted a perspective that I still use today with great effect. When that was blended with John Campbell's balanced approach customers began to achieve so much more. John, you've also been gone for a while, since 2004, but your teachings remain alive and well, thriving. Thank you for your insights and influence.

There have been a number of executives at various companies who have taught me a great deal about speaking their language and what it takes to get this important topic to the right audience and in the right way. One in particular stands out. He has had more influence than he probably realizes – Jim Gowans, a distinguished mining executive who currently serves on a number of boards has been a client several times. As a favor, Jim wrote the Foreword for this book. Together we've leveraged what I talk about in this book delivering results again and again. He really "gets it" and puts it into practice. It's about collaboration among functional groups who often work in silos and encouraging the leadership of those groups to work together. It is now crystal clear that it is open-minded leaders who can rock the boat, encourage collaboration and never let up, who are needed most. Without their persistence and big picture view, companies will always struggle to get past their own systemic dysfunction. Along the way, I've watched what he does, seen him get astounding results, and learned a great deal from him – thank you Jim.

The combined influence of John Campbell (maintenance is really about people), John Moubray (reliability is really about consequences), and Jim Gowans (results are really about collaboration) has been powerful. They have had a multiplier effect on my thinking and it is shared here.

As an individual I've needed help to be more whole. It's not all about work, it's about energy, preserving confidence and continually growing. There are three individuals who have helped a great deal with advice on managing my time, encouragement to do what I love, turn my natural skills and passions into something useful, and to stop slaving at tasks that drain my energy. Their coaching, facilitation and occasional kick in the pants have done wonders. I am now learning to do what energizes and avoid what drains me. To Dan Sullivan, creator of Strategic Coach, Candice McGarvey at Her Dollars, and Jamie Cornehlsen, our EOS implementer at Fitter Financials, a big thank you for your approach, your tools, for being there, for teaching, for coaching, and for watching my back.

I would also like to thank my many (hundreds if not more) colleagues, consultants, clients, students and friends worldwide who have worked with me, inspired me with their ideas and helped me learn in ways they may not even realize.

All of you are the people I learn from and to whom I owe a debt of gratitude. It's my hope that by sharing here, your wisdom goes even further.

James Reyes-Picknell

Foreword

I first met Jim Reyes-Picknell in Toronto in the late 1990's. He was delivering reliability training for our Canadian gold mines. I was VP of Operations, learning from him about how machinery and plant equipment fails, what we can do to avoid those failures and avoid the unwanted consequences they bring. Our mines latched onto the ideas and started to apply them – it helped our production. His advice about maintenance at a couple of the mines was a bit hard to swallow, but it paid off to follow it.

A few years later, I was working as VP Operations at a large nickel operation in Indonesia. We were struggling with production and equipment problems and well behind on production targets. With Jim's help we increased to nameplate and beyond achieving nearly 50% increase in production over the next couple of years and all of it through a focus on maintenance and reliability.

Several years later, I was being appointed as Managing Director of a large diamond mining operation in southern Africa. I called Jim with a now familiar request – can you help us, things are a mess there. He helped again. I've been impressed by the results he gets with his focus on maintenance, a key activity that is often poorly understood, overlooked, and under-appreciated.

During those efforts, Jim didn't shy away from telling me what he felt I needed to know. Even if he knew he was going counter to what I was thinking or about to do, he speaks up. In Africa he helped me avoid a decision about manpower that could potentially have had disastrous effects on our output. He showed me an alternative approach that would help us improve as we gradually reduced manpower through attrition. He's a straight shooter and as a consultant who truly has his customer's best interests at heart.

This book describes both the business benefits of doing the right things the right way, and an overview of how they are achieved. He focuses on efficiency in maintenance and effectiveness of the work being performed. The result, as I've seen, is higher reliability that translates in increases in production, enhancements to safety, lowering of operating risks and better overall financial performance.

This book is aimed at the senior executive who needs high performance from his or her physical assets and is struggling to achieve it. It's written in an easy to read style. It should be easy for financial, operational and other non-technical executives to understand. He's kept it short so you can probably read the whole thing during a 2 hour flight.

There are a lot of gems in this book. In these days of increased public pressure to operate safely and clean, regulatory oversight, shareholder pressure, increased public awareness of industrial risks, holding senior executives accountable for what goes wrong in their companies, and bad news that travels ultra- fast, this is a must read.

James K Gowans

Preface

This book was inspired by two events. The first was a remark that my book, "Uptime – Strategies for Excellence in Maintenance Management[1]" (Uptime) is a great reference book, but perhaps too in-depth as a text book for basic courses on managing maintenance. The second came from a growing realization that we needed to get our message to economic decision makers to whom reliability and maintenance people report.

Over the years since "Uptime" was first published (1995), there has been demand by maintainers for more detail and more depth. The second (2006) and third editions (2015) provided that. The book grew considerably. As a reference text it serves well, but for someone new to the field or in need of understanding the field without the details, it is often too much to assimilate easily. For non-maintainers however, "Uptime", is just too much.

In "Uptime" there are summaries at the back of each chapter. If you read the introduction, you'll know to look for them, but non-maintenance people, probably won't even read the introduction. The concepts that comprise those summaries form the basis for some of the content of this book. The decision maker who is often a non-technical boss of the maintainer, often in production or operations management, executive or general management role has other needs. They do need to know what maintenance should be delivering for the organization, a little bit about how it does that, and why it is important or they may be missing opportunities. With a bit of that knowledge, the decision maker can set expectations for the reliability and maintenance manager and for themselves.

---

[1] "Uptime – Strategies for Excellence in Maintenance Management", 3rd edition, J D Campbell and J V Reyes-Picknell, 2015, Productivity Press, NY

This book is written for the non-maintenance manager – the production, operational or financial manager and executives who would benefit from knowing what to expect from reliability and maintenance and from your technical staff who look after it for you.

Introduction

Your role is General Manager, Vice President of Operations, Chief Operating Officer or Chief Financial Officer. Your company it capital intensive and your physical assets are not performing as you'd like. Perhaps they've suffered years of abuse or neglect. You need reliable operations and that means you need to turn the situation around, as quickly as possible, and with as little investment as possible. As one friend, Paul Daoust puts it, you've got a "short runway" on which to take off and make this thing fly. You are in a tough spot and this book is for you.

Now change roles for a moment. If you were an investor with an opportunity to invest someone else's money, make back the investment within a year, earn multiples of that investment every year from then onwards, would you invest? At first you might think that's too good to be true, and in many cases, you'd be right. But in a capital intensive operation, you might just be dead wrong. It is possible to create this very scenario with your physical assets. Investing in them in such a way that the investment will earn multiples every year onwards. This is likely your case, because in truth, only a few companies manage their physical assets well today.

In a capital intensive industry, you or your company have already invested heavily in physical assets and depend on them to generate earnings. You may not know a lot about reliability and maintenance. You may think maintenance is about fixing things – and that's only correct when you break them. Maintenance real purpose is to avoid that situation wherever practical. It's really about getting the most out of those physical assets. In many companies, this means getting far more than you get today and you can do it at lower cost than you spend today maintaining them. Returns can be big, and the more "reactive" your operating environment is today, the higher its costs are and the bigger the prize for sorting it out. In fact the more reliable an operation is, the lower its costs to maintain and operate, the safer and less likely it is to suffer environmental excursions.

Physical asset maintenance and asset management projects can easily pay their way through big gains in productive time and cost savings. Unfortunately, there seem to be far too few outside of the fields of maintenance and asset management that fully realize this. Moreover, there are few in the field with sufficient business background to articulate the benefits, find the support they need to make improvements, and then execute them successfully. Too often, they are wrapped up in the day-to-day challenges.

If you are an investor, a production manager, or you are in one of the roles mentioned earlier, then you probably don't have a maintenance or reliability background. Even relatively few engineers have it. This book is for non-technical managers and executives who are involved in production and operational leadership roles. If you are an investor in such an operation, then you want to get them to read this. There is a lot of money on the table, much of it is left there and all because the decision makers don't even know it's there. You could be one of those decision makers, and I'm hoping to help you see and grab that money.

Reliability and maintenance people are generally good at the execution of their work, but they are often not very good at effectively communicating why they want to make the changes they need to make, and the organizational benefits that will result. On the other hand, decision makers (to whom the technical folks report) often don't have the background and understanding to make the connection themselves. Consequently, reliability and maintenance managers may know they have problems and even what to do about them, but fail to get the needed investment in resources of time and budget to make those changes. When this happens, there's been a break in communications. The economic buyer – to whom they report, may not even realize that there is an opportunity or problem.

This book begins by focusing on where value is created by the physical assets and how we manage them to deliver the highest value to the organization. It provides various examples of how reliability can be used to benefit various businesses and industries. Then it speaks to the various components of the "Uptime Pyramid of Excellence". The level of detail is fairly light. It is intended to provide enough insight into what should be happening, but not so much as to overwhelm a non-maintenance reader. Implementation (which depends heavily on senior management support) is discussed.

Quantification of benefits is possible and should be carried out on a case by case basis. Each situation is a bit different, so there's no one solution that can be shown. The approach however, is fairly uniform, drawing on your own data, or rules of thumb if the data at a given operation is lacking in the right details. It draws on benchmarks of what is achievable in various industries and operational environments. It can be applied at a single site or a portfolio of sites in a corporation or division.

We do not recommend attempting to determine this on your own – biases and egos can get in the way of an honest appraisal, and in many cases, knowledge of what "good" looks like is simply lacking. That appraisal requires a depth and breadth of knowledge of effective practices and their application for varying organizational objectives and constraints, and how those practices should interact. Even if you can determine, with confidence, the magnitude of cost savings and potential production gains, your in-house staff probably doesn't have a full understanding of the resources and internal efforts required to achieve them.

We have observed that the typical in-house efforts focus upon making small incremental changes, usually to gain efficiencies that provide some small cost savings, but do not go after the key changes that have significant impact on effectiveness and greatly improve organizational performance. It is almost as if making the effort is enough. There is sufficient skill and knowledge to identify and grab some of those small wins, however, the big ones usually remain untouched. In fairness, those probably entail some tough decisions and actions. Getting outside help is a good approach but it needs to be the right help.

Where in-house staff have estimated the costs associated with getting good outside help, they are often way off the mark. Aside from creating a budget hurdle to making change happen, those under-estimates of costs, when combined with overly conservative estimates of the potential benefits, can kill the initiative. Perhaps, there is sub-conscious resistance to change that can lead to avoidance of the need to deal with the tough steps that are likely to be required.

Unless your staff have successfully worked in a senior consulting role helping organizations to make these changes, they are unlikely to have that breadth and depth of knowledge to successfully make the required changes. This is especially the case when it comes to organizational change leadership and management. Organizations are usually good at doing what they do to deliver a given product or service. Doing so consistently requires consistency of action. If improvement is needed, a change in that action is needed. Managers, by their nature won't make those changes, especially if they are dramatic. Managers don't do change well. You need leaders and in today's businesses, we see a dearth of leadership – we are usually over-managed.

We've observed that unsuccessful in-house change efforts usually leave the organization unwilling to try again. They've tried, failed and then moved on to other opportunities, without a full evaluation of why they failed. That can negatively impact the organization for quite a while, even years. A familiar remark by those in companies where we've been asked to help out is that "we've tried that before" – it just won't work here. Consequently, any further efforts will then need to overcome significant hurdles created by the past failures. The awareness and experience with this very dynamic, that comes with experienced change leaders and specialized outside help are usually the answer.

Efficiency and Effectiveness

From an operational perspective, there are two targets when improving performance in physical asset maintenance: efficiency and effectiveness. Each delivers value albeit to a limited extent if they are not combined. There is a multiplier effect that arises when dealing with both in tandem. Sadly, relatively few companies take full advantage of that and pay attention to both.

Perhaps the most common approach to improvements is to begin with some sort of assessment. It identifies areas of weakness (opportunities) where improvements can be made. The level of maturity of the organization is taken into account. Less mature organizations will usually start with the simpler improvements to processes and practices while the more advanced tackle the more complex.

Attempting to make improvement entirely "in-house" usually fails to achieve very much. Although the motivation can be high, the in-depth knowledge of "what good looks like" if often lacking. The bar is set low and results are mediocre.

Getting outside help solves that problem, but just who helps can really matter.

If a software company or a consultancy that helps to implement software are involved in the assessment process, then there is usually a lot of focus on the "maintenance system" in the information technology sense. The advisors stand to gain more from software license fees and the implementation project than they do from offering solid advice (if indeed they can). The result is that a lot of effort, money and time are expended to introduce software that just doesn't solve anything. These systems are often described, erroneously, as "solutions", yet they are really just tools.

Software isn't strategy! Where the primary focus is on software, the cart is truly before the horse.

There is no way that even a good computer system can add value if all it does is automate previously inefficient processes and ineffective practices. Of course some systems are indeed implemented very well, but even so, they can only help with work management and related processes leading to greater efficiency at work execution. Most of the available computer systems for managing maintenance are rather hopeless for reliability (effectiveness) improvement.

If reliability is the initial focus, yet other (work and materials management) processes are not mature, then those efforts will deliver limited to no results. Indeed there are many companies that have attempted reliability improvements and been disappointed with the results of those efforts. Their focus on effectiveness alone disappoints. What's worse, they often leave the company with a sense that they cannot improve, so they give up.

Most companies prefer to tackle improvements in small stages. Rarely do we see a holistic approach that focuses on the entire spectrum of activities needed to achieve maximum value. A broad program need not be implemented all at once though – it too can be dealt with in logical steps. The next chapter that deals with value will explain that. First however, we need to understand some basics about efficiency and effectiveness. We need to think more holistically, less tactically and more strategically.

The stage is set by speaking to efficiency and effectiveness – the two most important keys to maximizing value in an operational (production or service delivery) environment where there is a heavy reliance on your capital investment in physical assets to perform.

The table shown in figure 1 compares and contrasts the two concepts of efficiency and effectiveness.

	Efficiency	Effectiveness
Meaning	The virtue of being efficient. Miserly use of resources.	The magnitude of nearness of the actual to the intended result.
What does it mean in Maintenance?	Doing work the right way and at the right time without error.	Doing the right work that produces the greatest result.
Places emphasis on	Inputs and outputs - costs and completion.	Methods and outcomes delivering the greatest value.
Time horizon	Short term	Long term
Approach	Narrow focus within department	Holistic, with broad based cross functional collaboration
How do we get there?	Implementing strategy	Formulating strategy
Leadership/Sponsorship	Functional / Departmental or Site	Corporate / Executive
Focus is on...	Operational activities	Business outcomes

Figure 1 Efficiency and Effectiveness Compared

Efficiency derives from executing a number of tactical activities with the least expenditure of resources (money, labor, etc.). In physical asset maintenance, one common area for improvement in efficiency is the planning of work to be performed so that it can be done in the least time. Another improvement derives from scheduling the work when it will disrupt production the least. Yet another is the provision of parts to support maintenance work in a timely manner. These and other activities all result in saved money (reduced expense) to the business. Often though, even the combining of improvements in two mutually dependent areas is seldom tackled. Maintenance planning (forecasting demand) and materials support (satisfying that demand) are often tackled independently of each other if only because they managed by different departments with different priorities.

Let's assume that those two are being improved, and to-gether. If the planning is for repair work and it is being performed in response to breakdowns that disrupt operations, then there is room to improve further. Breakdowns are difficult to forecast so demand forecasting will be challenging. To compensate for that, parts and materials stores will be over-stocked of "just-in-case" items.

However, in many cases, breakdowns need not be disruptive and need not result in loss of output. Proactive maintenance can be performed to avoid them or time the needed repairs, just be-fore the breakdowns occur so that disruption can be minimized. The more proactive the work being performed is, the more accu-rate materials demands can be forecast too. To achieve that requires a focus on doing the right maintenance – being more ef-fective.

Planning, scheduling, demand forecasting, materials provi-sion and defining the right proactive work to perform must all be done together to generate the most value. The total value gener-ated is greater than the sum of its parts – usually by a large margin.

Many organizations today still manage both maintenance and reliability in very traditional ways and underperform. It's really obvious if they have a "break-then-fix" approach. That is repre-sented by the lower left quadrant in figure 2.

In that situation, their failures to plan and schedule will be obvious to the trades, who are usually quite frustrated. They won't be able to start and finish jobs without interruption, they will need to make multiple trips to the storeroom, suffer near con-tinual interruptions from other "emergencies," and experience a lot of waiting around.

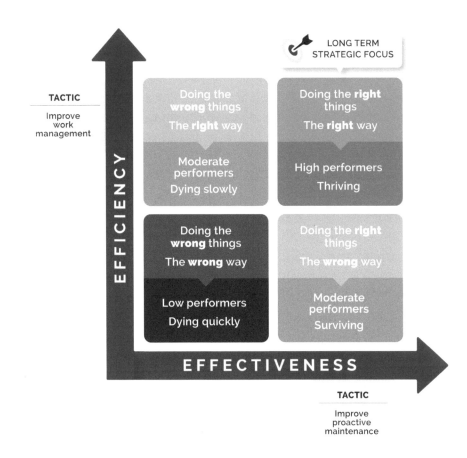

Figure 2 Mapping where you are

In those cases they usually know they are performing poorly. We often find that the maintenance managers in those cases have come up from the tools. They are focused on field improvements that show up in how work is executed - work management, planning, scheduling and parts supply. Those improvements will take time because there is a lot of old and often dysfunctional behavior to change. They are on the right track and will eventually improve efficiency. As that happens, there will be a bit more wrench time and they can then get to the proactive maintenance that has probably been ignored because of the past breakdown experience. If they do that, then they may also see some gains in reliability.

Improving on the identification of proactive work requires some advanced knowledge of reliability methods and tools. Those capabilities are often missing in organizations in the lower left quadrant. Consequently, due to the lack of knowledgeable resources, those improvements are often tackled later, if at all. In fact, when organizations see improvement based solely on work management, they are often satisfied and tend to stop there.

Where there are those who understand reliability, the organization may begin to increase focus on proactive programs – getting the PMs done. Often they'll look to manufacturer's recommendations, not a bad starting point, but not the best either.

If they stop there they will see benefit, but they could probably see a lot more. Without additional effort to identify the right work to be done, their performance gains will be somewhat limited. In figure 2, they would be in the upper left quadrant – doing some wrong things, but doing them well.

Some organizations are quite technically oriented. They tend to have strong "engineering" cultures. They may even have engineers in senior roles. The focus there will almost always be on technology and engineering approaches. Those organizations are very capable of identifying the right work to do if they accept the established methods. However, if they've viewed the problem as being essentially technical in nature, and tackled the task of improving reliability as such, then they are likely to also fail at achieving top results.

They will increase effectiveness to a degree, but without the work management improvement, they will only move to the lower right quadrant, doing the right things the wrong way. Effort is required in both areas, involving technical, process and people elements. In reliability, a shift in thinking is also required – it's not about the assets and failures, it's really about identifying and managing risks to minimize consequences of failures.

Doing that will move the organization to the upper right quadrant doing the right things the right way. The management of work and its execution are maximizing available wrench time and workforce utilization. By doing the right proactive maintenance unexpected failures are avoided and consequences are managed. Risks are also mitigated. Costs are lower. Output capacity is higher. Morale is better among both operators and maintainers. The organization is on its way to being a high performer.

This book is about moving to that upper right quadrant, and doing it as quickly as possible.

The business results attained will depend on which quadrant you sustain. If your business is low margin or struggling with difficult markets, then you could be in trouble and you need to be in the high performance quadrant – you can't afford not to be there. With high margins and lots of demand, unless you are in that same upper right quadrant you could be doing better. Profitability is increased if your physical asset maintenance is both efficient and effective.

The next chapter describes what needs to be done to achieve those two goals – efficiency and effectiveness together to achieve the maximum value. More-over, there is a trick to obtaining rapid results from reliability improvement efforts with relatively little focus on efficiency, treating problematic assets as special cases. In our experience, those improvements often have big financial impact and provide sufficient payback to fund all of the improvement efforts in maintenance and reliability and usually very quickly.

Where's the value?

Benjamin Franklin's axiom, "An ounce of prevention is worth a pound of cure", has been used most commonly when referring to health care. It is also highly appropriate in reliability and maintenance circles. We do take care of the health of our physical assets after all!

In health care we don't really look at the costs of doing regular exercise nor the health "repairs" avoided. In business we do. We want to know what the prevention will cost, and what we will save by avoiding the cost of the cure. On top of that, we often want guarantees that our efforts will in fact be rewarded.

In the reliability world we know that effective maintenance practices resulting in high reliability will be beneficial to our companies. In many cases, improving performance will cost a fraction of the money potentially saved and an even smaller fraction of the production or output to be gained. Yet, most M&R (Maintenance & Reliability) practitioners cannot seem to effectively articulate the financial value of the work done, nor explain just what financial benefits can be achieved by doing it. The reliability folks often don't really see what they are really there to do – manage consequences of failures, not necessarily the failures themselves. Those in risk management look at that, but all too often they lack the technical knowledge of reliability needed to fully appreciate what's happening to create those risks.

Management information systems are not often set up in a way that helps us either. We need to dig to find costs that are often reported in the wrong or catch-all accounts. Benefits are not tracked in accounting systems at all. Consider that savings are costs you don't spend, and therefore you don't account for them. Increased revenues are accounted for, but only as revenues, perhaps by product line or brand. Attributing them to specific improvements, especially if many are being undertaken, is a challenge that few can, or are willing to tackle.

Even though we know there will be benefits from doing the right things, these days we need to justify by showing a return on the investment of those improvement costs. We were recently asked by a major client to show them how we would measure value delivered by their improvement program in maintenance and reliability. They wanted to assure themselves that they were spending their money wisely.

New projects and Life Cycle Economics

In most industries, private and public sector, new construction projects get a lot of attention. They require massive up-front investments of capital, take time to design, build, commission and only then, sometimes years later, will they produce a return on that investment. We've all heard of "return on investment" (ROI) in which project payback is maximized by getting the most revenue once operations commence and keeping project costs and durations as low as possible. Most companies have payback hurdle rates that must be exceeded in order to secure the capital funding needed for the project. Zealous project leaders will do their best to lower capital investment costs and get the project delivered early, all to maximize ROI.

The flaw with this is that ROI, while seemingly long term in focus (5 or 10 years perhaps), really isn't a great yardstick. It is far too easily manipulated to make the project look good on paper in order to secure funding. It does take future operating and maintenance costs into account, often as a factor. For example, maintenance might be assumed to fall in the range of 3% to 20% of operating costs. But that does not take into account reliability and asset performance degradation over time, and more importantly, its impact on loss of operational output.

To maximize ROI, a project manager can cut all sorts of corners – less training for future operators, no training for maintainers (they are usually forgotten), buy the lowest cost recommended spares package from equipment suppliers, accept the manufacturer's standard information packages, use cheapest available construction techniques and lowest costs contractors, etc. If reliability, maintainability and operability are not considered with dedicated studies during the project phases, then O&M costs will almost certainly be high. Failing to consider those results in difficulty operating and maintaining the plant, and often, an unreliable plant that needs a lot of maintenance intervention. Merely following building codes and long established design and construction standards is not enough. Just ask any maintainer or operator.

As the asset ages beyond its original ROI time horizon, say 10 years, the asset will be deteriorating naturally with use. It will become more costly to maintain. The company has recouped its capital investment, yet still wants the asset to perform – after all, it is now producing profitable revenues if it is can be operated and maintained cost effectively. While the time value of money will make those future costs less relevant in the project ROI calculations, it will not make those costs irrelevant when operating the plant 10 years hence. If those costs are high the asset may be less economical to operate, but if there's no money to invest in replacement assets you will want it to continue. A bit more upfront investment in reliability, maintainability and operability studies, in determining the best maintenance program and sparing strategies, really pays off as the asset ages.

In the mining industry for example, the mine itself is a depleting asset – its value goes down as you mine the ore. Often the ore grades also go down, but rising commodity prices make them attractive, if O&M costs are favorable, then the mine can economically extract those lesser ore grades, extend the remaining life of the mine and turn otherwise unrecoverable ore into reserves on the balance sheet increasing the value of the company.

Other industries face similar situations – an older plant that can be run cost effectively can compete with more modern facilities elsewhere. Keeping it in a state to perform that well however, requires a substantial investment in asset management, something that the original ROI for a project would rarely, if ever, consider.

In Canada we have one of the world's most cost competitive integrated steel mills, and that's in an environment with high labor and energy costs. Parts of that mill are over 60 years old and most of it is over 40! Replacing that mill would require a $10 to 12 billion investment today. Its initial capital costs were recouped many years ago. Today, keeping it operating and profitable provides a huge value to the company that owns it – in fact it was able to perform as a cash cow to help fund improvements at various other mills in the parent company's portfolio.

Taking that sort of potential into account requires more than a simple ROI calculation on a project investment with a 10 year horizon. Return on Asset value (ROA) is a most holistic approach and it may well justify a greater capital investment at a lower ROI to achieve that longer term superior asset performance.

What can you do with more reliable assets?

Each industry is a bit different from others – some are private sector and profit motivated, private sector and regulated, or public sector.

Private Sector

Most of our business is with the private sector where there is an interest in profitability and returns for the companies' owners. They want to reduce the cost per unit of output. High reliability contributes to both lower costs and increased running times due to fewer failures. Moreover, it contributes to risk reduction and management. The proactive maintenance required to achieve high reliability is also achieved at lower costs than allowing failures to occur and repairing them. A reliable operation will be less expensive, more productive and lower risk.

If your business revenues are constrained by your production capacity then you really need reliability to be high.

If your business cannot sell everything it can produce it is said to be market constrained. In this situation your revenues are constrained and costs become a major focus. Reliable assets won't break down as often so your maintenance costs will be lowered. You can't however, use that additional availability to earn more revenue, but you can use it reduce other operating costs. If you can produce enough to meet market demands in a shorter time, then you can operate for shorter times – reducing shifts, shift lengths, or numbers of days you operate. You may be able to idle spare production capacity. All of those will reduce your variable costs of production and put less demand on maintenance resources. In these cases, reliability also helps your business increase its profits.

Regulated Industries

In the regulated environment (e.g.: most utilities) they really do need to contain costs while managing risks. Their top line (revenue) is often constrained by fixed rates and no flexibility to change them without complex and expensive regulatory processes. They may also need to allow for the high costs of regular regulatory rate reviews which ironically drive up the total costs that the regulators are attempting to contain. Reliability of physical assets means they will incur fewer failures, therefore fewer expensive repairs and less disruption to customer services. However, in most cases, revenues cannot be increased so the focus is solely on costs.

Pipelines may be an exception in the utility world. More throughput does mean more revenue. They are regulated heavily yet increased reliability means more availability and therefore increased flow volumes which can indeed generate revenues. In those cases the private sector, for profit motives can apply.

Of course regulations are different from one jurisdiction to another, and are set by lawmakers who have their own and their constituents' interests at heart. In some cases regulators tie rates to asset base, providing incentive to the utilities to increase capital investment rather than sustain long term performance of older assets. Utilities in this environment tend to minimize their focus on maintenance, being happy to achieve average results, while shortening the "life" of those assets through slow but progressive deterioration to the point where capital investment is required to replace them. While reliability improvements will help keep costs down, spending to achieve that there really is little to no incentive to keep the assets reliable.

Public Sector

In the public sector focus is often on service delivery at low cost. Public sector organizations don't tend to make heavy use of capital assets except for facilities and vehicle fleets. Budgets, not market, will determine what you can spend so you want to spend that budget where it will do the most good. Keeping costs down, as in the market constrained public sector is a benefit, and more rapid or efficient service delivery may matter. The times when services can be delivered are likely fixed but time savings in processing can be reduced, thereby increasing customer satisfaction. Unfortunately, coming in below budget is often seen as a bad thing – if a civil servant fails to spend budget, then next year's budget is likely reduced along with perceptions of how important the civil servant's role actually is. Sadly, the effects described by C. Northcote Parkinson[2] work against us in this sector. Reliability can

---

[2] Cyril Northcote Parkinson, "Parkinson's Law, or the Pursuit of Progress", 1955, The Economist. London, UK

certainly help where physical assets are used, but the benefits may be very difficult to quantify.

Health care may be private or public sector depending on jurisdiction. Their assets comprise large facilities with a number of complex installed systems and a large investment in bio-medical equipment. While costs are important, reliability is paramount. Unreliable equipment or even hotel services (e.g.: HVAC and elevators) in a hospital can result in unsafe conditions, risks to patient care and even fatalities.

Air Transport and Nuclear Power

The air transport industry is an excellent example of reliability. Indeed it is where reliability first moved from an engineering interest to public interest. Safety and customer service are of primary importance followed closely by cost. Nuclear power is similar. In those industries, high reliability is, and has long been recognized as the key to achieving all of those objectives.

Key Performance and Process Indicators

We could have showed them an array of key performance indicators (KPIs), but truth be told, they would have been largely smoke and mirrors. KPIs often focus on costs and results, both of which are indirectly controllable through your process actions. The process is where focus needs to be. Consider that reliability and maintenance are a process. The process has inputs and outputs:

Input → process → output.

- Inputs are what we spend money on – energy, labor, services, and materials.
- Outputs are what we get out of the process – its results. Results include increased uptime, reliability, and availability that enable increased production and/or service delivery, therefore increased revenue. It also lowers risk

while supporting safety performance and environmental compliance.

- The process in the middle uses the inputs to deliver the outputs. In addition to key performance indicators, we also need key process indicators (also KPIs).

In the reliability and maintenance (R&M) process there are in fact many sub-processes such as: work management, planning, scheduling, supervision, skills development, contracting, outsourcing, materials provision, stores, inventory management, root cause analysis, reliability centered maintenance, and proactive maintenance optimization.

Going beyond R&M into the realm of good asset management we also have evidence based decision making, Weibull analysis, reliability – availability – maintainability (RAM) analysis, Life Cycle Cost analysis, Total Life Cost analysis, etc.

Many of us in the field specialize in one or more of these various sub-processes and we tend to get a bit too wrapped up in them, failing to see the forest for the trees.

Many of us in these fields tend to specialize. We may have one or more areas of expertise in one or more of these many sub-processes. We are all technical people with a good eye for detail, very linear and logical thinking processes. Few of us have business school backgrounds or any sort of management, or executive training. Anyone who knows us, knows that we tend to get caught up in the technical details. While that is great for problem solving and analysis, it tends to blind us to the big picture.

On top of that, we have technological distractions, in the form of various information management (technology) IM/IT systems. While these are intended to help us, they often end up becoming the focus whilst distracting us with the sheer volume of data they hold. Never-the-less, some IT helps us with transactions and keeping track of the extensive details (work orders, purchasing, stores issues, returns, etc.). Some of it is somewhat automated and helps us with work flow and keeping on track with analytical processes like Root Cause Failure Analysis (RCFA), Reliability Centered Maintenance (RCM), spares calculations, etc. Some is aimed at helping us make sense of all the volume of data by helping us with data extraction, manipulation and reporting of Key Performance indicators.

KPIs are like score-boards in sports. The athletes do the work and the score board records the achievements (KPIs). Those scores alone, have no value but they tell us a lot about what does. They must drive changed performance – more wins and more valuable prizes. In maintenance and reliability we put a lot of effort into measuring with our KPIs (our score boards), but often we put far too little effort into the behaviors that get us those scores.

IT / IM complexity requires a great deal of investment. Considering how distracted and ill-informed we are by technology, I'd argue that much of that investment is misplaced.

We truly do tend to be enamored with technology these days. We expect that by installing it, we will see benefits. The IT sales persons do nothing to dispel that. On the contrary, they take advantage of our general lack of sophistication. The rest of us who are non-IT people, tend to be somewhat gullible too – we actually believe the sales pitches because we desperately want them to be true. Now however, after a couple of decades of heavy IT investment that has shown little real return, we've grown more skeptical. Increasingly we are seeing IT as the enabler that it is and less as a "solution".

So, where does a company put its money and where does it see the best payback? If it's not IT, when where does the value arise? That payback must come from somewhere in the physical assets, the processes (the things you do) and people (the ones who do it). We are realizing now, perhaps slowly, that IT investment needs to be more focused on helping the people be more efficient at managing and working the business process that drive value from those assets.

The following graphic (figure 3) shows relationships between the major activities needed to lower costs and increase outputs, and how they interact to generate value. Value is measured as O&M $ / unit of output. We achieve greatest value from a focus on efficiency and effectiveness in parallel.

The activities on the right contribute more output, those on the left reduce cost. In combination they optimize the output. There's no start point because all these activities are likely in place already in most organizations. Each of them could use improvement, and for maximum value overall, those improvements should be coordinated.

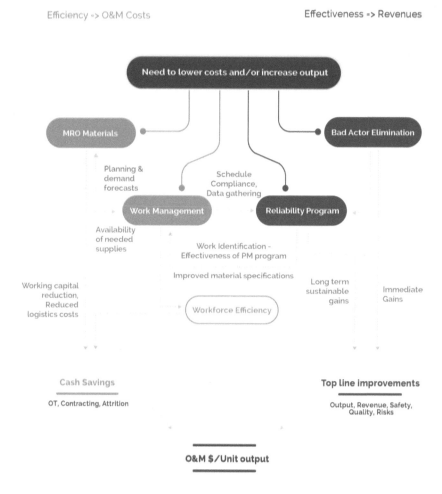

Figure 3 **Where value arises from reliability and efficient maintenance and MRO materials management practices**

Some value derives from efficient execution of the work and material support processes. That helps to drive costs down. Greater value, in the form of increased output, derives from a reliable operation that can run longer, producing more product. In turn that requires the right proactive maintenance to be done. If there are known problems with reliability, those can be solved quickly (bad actor elimination). Once solutions to those problems are identified, they must be executed in the work management processes. Once control over operations is attained – it is less reactive, then the reliability program can optimize it. The diagram doesn't show timing, but it should be fairly evident that there are some dependencies among the various activities that, depending on where you begin, could impact on how any particular organization times its improvement program activities.

The result of this value chain in Figure 3 is "operations and maintenance cost per unit of output". Ultimately that's what companies are looking for – cost effectiveness. By increasing margin on sales with reduced costs, and increasing Output / Revenue, we increase profitability.

Other benefits include much better maintenance budget forecast accuracy, budget compliance, and much better forecasting of production volumes and revenues.

Each of the various improvement activities shown in the figure creates value at different times throughout an improvement project's implementation. Some of the benefit arises fairly quickly, usually from early reliability efforts, and some much later from a sustained focus on efficiency of maintenance and supporting spare parts practices.

Quantifying the benefits from an improvement initiative involving all these activities can be challenging, especially if the management systems set up for maintenance and operational performance do not link costs to assets and their performance. However, quantification of benefits is possible and the costs to achieve them fairly easily estimated. Those costs are often a small fraction of the total benefit to be gained, making the improvement initiative self-financing, often within the first year.

Recently we developed a business case for an improvement initiative across six operational locations in several countries. Aggregated savings due to efficiency gains were nearly $100 million per year and aggregated production gains due to the effectiveness of reliability programs were worth nearly $1 billion a year. In combination those benefits were roughly the equivalent of the investment required to build an entirely new production site. In their case, the investment required to get that benefit was less than $20 million, spread over a two to three year period!

The Uptime Pyramid of Excellence

In my 2015 book, "Uptime – Strategies for Excellence in Maintenance Management", there is a "Pyramid of Excellence" divided into three parts: Leadership, Essentials and Choosing Excellence. Managers keep the boat steady – they are incented to produce steady and stable results, not to change things. Leaders, by contrast, rock the boat – they make change happen. Hopefully that change is for the good. The Uptime Pyramid of Excellence (Figure 4) is a model representing effective practices. It comprises 10 components grouped into three tiers: leadership, essentials and choosing excellence. They build on each other and as maturity increases in each level it enables even higher performance at the levels above. Uptime is about throwing the least amount of money at the problem to achieve high performance.

Leadership, the first level, is foundational – you can manage and run a maintenance department without leadership, but you will struggle to change its performance. As a leader, you must make changes, those will rock the boat and that will spark all sorts of resistance and challenge. Change Leadership is needed, not just change management. In fact, in light of the differences between leaders and managers, one might consider the term "change management" to be somewhat of an oxymoron.

Figure 4 Uptime Pyramid of Excellence

Essentials are on the second tier. These are components of managing maintenance that you will almost certainly have in place already, whether you are managing a high or low performing maintenance department. In fact what our consultants see quite often is that all these essential components are in place, but performance in all of them is lacking. Complaints that parts are unavailable when needed, work isn't performed on schedule or delivered as promised, planning is inadequate or missing, schedule compliance requires a schedule to begin with, there are few meaningful performance measures, systems that distract with data rather than inform, and more, are all signs that these essentials are being mismanaged.

Combined, and when done well, they help the maintenance department be efficient – getting work done quickly, on schedule and at lowest practical cost. Changing them to improve performance will require changes to behaviors and habits that are often deeply embedded. You will require some insight into why you are performing the way you are today, and then you will need both the will and leadership to instigate change.

Choosing excellence is the top tier and it is named to reflect that excellence is not a destination, but a journey. Mediocre performers often do poorly at the essentials and have little focus on this tier which is all about the effectiveness of the work you do. Effectiveness demands that you do the right work, not just do work well. Effectiveness of your maintenance program is what drives reliability achievement. Combined with high performance in the essentials you can deliver amazing results. If the essentials are still being mismanaged, improvements aimed at reliability at this top tier will produce disappointing results.

The following three sections provide an overview of what each of the Uptime components is all about. Understand these and you will have a good sense of what your reliability and maintenance managers should be doing. However, you might be short on time, or your interest may be more directly on how to use Uptime to achieve improved results. In that case, then skip to Implementation. If your interest is in quantifying benefits, then skip to Your Business Case for Change.

Leadership

Leadership is the foundation of good reliability and maintenance management. As a rule, managers are good at keeping things stable. They can't manage their way to high performance, but they will sustain it once it is achieved. You need leadership to get you there.

Achieving higher levels of performance will require changed behavior, that requires changed thinking, and all that change requires leadership. The leadership level of the Uptime Pyramid is a needed enabler for the organization to develop competence at the Essentials and to ever having a hope of Choosing Excellence. You are paying for your people and management already, you might as well get the most value from your investment.

Management systems are set up to sustain performance using predictable, repeatable and consistent processes. Managers keep those systems and processes working – in simple terms, they "keep the boat steady". Implementing improvements through "Uptime" requires leadership, someone must be willing to rock the boat and accept all the angst and ridicule that will come from those who do not want it, and will therefore resist it.

"It ought to be remembered that there is nothing more difficult to take in hand, more perilous to conduct, or more uncertain in its success, than to take the lead in the introduction of a new order of things. Because the innovator has for enemies all those who have done well under the old conditions, and lukewarm defenders in those who may do well under the new. This coolness arises partly from fear of the opponents, who have the laws on their side, and partly from the incredulity of men, who do not readily believe in new things until they have had a long experience of them." Niccolo Machiavelli in "The Prince".

These days our businesses tend to be over-managed and under-led. Ask anyone who sees the need for change, the inflexibility of business processes and systems, and the reluctance on the part of management (sometimes mistakenly called, leadership), to implement any form of change. Business schools teach management, not leadership. Leaders are not necessarily managers nor are they necessarily in manager roles. Your initiative to improve performance will require leadership, best if applied at the top. Those who are too junior will likely be subordinate to other managers, even in other functional areas or departments, who will resist the change.

Strategy

In the Lewis Carroll book, "Alice in Wonderland," the Cheshire Cat said, "If you don't know where you are going, any road will get you there." Perhaps organizations should pay attention too. Many today are meandering aimlessly, following any road ahead, without thought as to the end result and what they want to achieve.

Leadership sets direction and that direction is a high level plan of action – a strategy. Your strategy needs to be clearly defined, communicated effectively, and seen as achievable. It will have a vision of your future state and goals that will be recognizable when you get there. The strategy is a high level and broad strokes plan – not too detailed, but with sufficient guidance for decisions on what to do next. It provides criteria for decision making when there are not rules for all potential scenarios. The details are developed for each component of your strategy and each of those, deals with a challenge or an opportunity.

In choosing excellence, you will be choosing a path of constant change and improvement. That is not something you can simply manage. Leadership is about vision and direction (strategy), its effective execution and your people – arguably the most critical element. Taking your organization from "good" to "better" to "great," or from "ordinary" to "extraordinary," or "average" to "exceptional", requires direction. You need a clear idea of what extraordinary looks like, a sense of where you are now and a plan to close the gap, and the commitment to making it happen. Making those changes can be a complex process and it won't come without some angst and pain. Good leaders are there to rock the boat, managers keep it stable – this dichotomy sets you up for conflict which must be contained.

Maintenance as a part of your Strategy

Maintenance is a critical business function. It consumes both fixed and variable costs and pays you back with productive capacity to create value for the organization. We don't often think that expenses have a payback, but this one does. Reducing maintenance costs through efficiency gains (doing maintenance the right way) and effectiveness (doing the right things) increases operating margins. Maintenance also contributes substantially to the company's safety and environmental performance and its overall risk profile as viewed by financial and insurance institutions. Consider that accidents on the job often involve maintainers and systems that are not performing properly. Environmental problems are a result of leaks, lack of containment, poorly operating emissions controls. Many of your business risks are a direct result of the potential for plant and equipment to fail.

Well-maintained assets meet production commitments easily and at lower risk, something that lenders and insurers like to see. When building a new plant, consider the importance of maintenance and reliability. Decisions made at the design stage provide you with the greatest opportunity, by far, to optimize Return on Asset Investment (ROA) by reducing total life-cycle operating and maintenance costs, and ensure high sustained performance and benefits. Maintenance strategy and the details of your maintenance program (perhaps better called your reliability program) are most easy to define in these "greenfield" scenarios, yet often ignored. Successful operations don't wait until they are in commissioning and starting new operations to figure out what they should be doing to keep the plant operational. They understand that the Operating and Maintenance phase of the assets is the longest period in the asset lifetime, has the highest total costs, and is key in determining the profitability of the organization.

Keep it simple

Strategy should be kept simple. Your business objectives, the business and asset environment, its present state, and the state of maintenance management practices are your starting points. Understand what it means to be a high performer and using effective practices – what "good" looks like. Training in Uptime is an excellent starting point. You won't learn "best practices" anywhere – whatever is best for your company is what works best for your company, not necessarily what is "best" for others. There are many "effective" practices in the Uptime Pyramid, but there are no universally "best" practices.

Based on your organizational strategic direction, decide what you want to achieve—that is your "vision." Look at performance and practices today – they are good indicators of your ability to achieve your vision. If performance today is disappointing, then you will need to change your thinking and behavior. Consider what effective practices, such as those described in *Uptime*, will be the best to help you close any gaps. Develop a plan of action to implement those improvements. Plan the broad brush strokes for the entire initiative. Don't be surprised if it takes a few years to complete in an existing operation. Detail that plan for the first year and begin implementing. Execution is what matters.

When you have a strategy defined, or even just coming together, you'll want a program charter. The charter will define what you are aiming to do, by when, how, and how it will be measured and managed through the transition. It also sets the foundation for the longer term governance to ensure your new process, methods and expectations "stick" after you've finished making them.

Avoid the temptation to plan the details for years in advance. Along the way you will run into difficulties that cannot be foreseen today. In 1880, Prussian military commander Helmuth van Moltke wrote, "No plan of operations reaches with any certainty beyond the first encounter with the enemy's main force." He was very insightful and his wisdom applies to any plan. Limit the detailed planning to shorter horizons and update it as you move along.

Governance and Sustaining Your Improvements

Good governance of your improvement initiative and integration of it with other improvement programs are essential. To avoid conflicts and competition for resources, use a technique like the lean method, "Hoshin Kanri" to deploy your strategy. Ideally that process begins at the corporate level so that your maintenance vision is driven by a clear sense of where the organization is going and how it is going to get there.

In some cases, you may choose to outsource maintenance. Do it for the right reasons. It is not a way to unload responsibility. Transferring a "problem" to someone else may not be the answer. If done poorly it can even be harmful. If maintenance is of strategic importance or if it is unique to your business, you are probably better off keeping it in-house. Otherwise outsourcing may be a good option – a company specialized in maintenance may be better at it than you are, considering that it is not your primary business focus.

Once you have embarked on making improvements, it is important to sustain them. Excellence as described in "Uptime" is a journey, not a destination. Don't rush it, sustain the pressure to improve and never let up. Annual reviews of your strategic plans, tactical deployment activities and progress are essential elements to keeping on track with your journey. You will know it is working when you find yourself dealing with new challenges every year and not revisiting the same ones.

People and Teams

Helen Keller said, "Alone we can do so little, together we can do so much". You and your people need to be skilled, knowledgeable, motivated and all "pulling their oars in the same direction". Deployment of your strategic plan, the various projects it will include, and ongoing execution of your maintenance or asset management system (and we don't mean information technology) requires the right quantity of the right people, suitably motivated and rewarded to achieve your strategic goals. As Jim Collins describes in "Good to Great[3]", you need the right people on the bus and you need them in the right seats!

Execution of your strategy, or even keeping the boat steady will only happen through people – nothing else. People are an important, arguably the most important, strategic asset you've got to work with. You cannot provide solid leadership without people to lead nor manage a complex business function without people with the right skills, knowledge and motivation. If you think about it, you already have people. Making sure they are the right people and in the right roles, trained and skilled to the levels you need, is a small incremental cost with potentially huge benefits.

An organization is an extension of its people. It stands to reason that we need to focus on people if we want our organizations to thrive and evolve. Both you and your people need to make the choice to take this journey together and for each-others benefit, not just for the company, its profits, or its shareholders. After all, you are the ones on the bus, not the shareholders! Narrow visions focused only on the business as a money making entity, will cripple your efforts to improve. Except for the shareholders, who are not really on this journey with you, no one really cares about

---

[3] Jim Collins, "Good to Great, Why Some Companies Make the Leap and Some Don't", 2001, Harper Business, NY

the business making money. They care about what is in it for them.

Changing from where you are to where you want to go, will require effort focused on the change. It will be critical to success but it should not be a separate project work-stream running in parallel with your improvement efforts. "Change management" is not just a human resources, marketing or internal communications exercise, although those are a part of it.

When we go into a store we are often there to "buy" something we want, not to be "sold" something we do not want. It doesn't work to sell your program to your people – you want them to want it so that they will buy it. They must want it. People are actually very good at handling change whenever it is their idea to change, but they will resist if you try to impose change on them. Change management, or from the perspective of those undergoing the change, "change ownership", must be an integral part of all you do – built into every activity and communication. Excellence is a journey where change will be constant – you need to be good at handling the people, process, technical, physical and emotional aspects that come with change.

As a senior executive it is your role to direct the organization, but you cannot simply mandate change, give orders and expect to get results. People just don't follow orders very well any more. Technical people are often not the best "people – people". They are logical and can be lacking in emotional intelligence, particularly when it comes to dealing with others. Purely technical approaches, the long-time favorites of engineers and technical people, don't work well. Installing a new computerized management system is not a "solution" nor will it guarantee success. View technology as a tool, it has a big cost and no payback, don't put it in place and expect problems to melt away. Look instead to your people for the answers you need and you will do well.

Effective managers today are not likely to be purely technical people. Rising through the ranks on the basis of technical merit alone is common-place and it is a recipe for poor management. Imagine promoting your best mechanic who loves to get his hands on your equipment but doesn't get along well with others into a supervisory role. You've just lost a good mechanic and created a bad supervisor.

Choose your managers on the basis of their suitability for the role they are heading into, not on the basis of past performance or technical merit alone. You need a balance of technical, managerial, leadership and human skills.

Organizational Design

Organizational designs continue to evolve and even cycle. Centralized, military style organizations give way to more responsive decentralized structures. To deliver maximum business benefits, traditional maintenance, engineering and operations departments are working together under the umbrella of "Asset Management". Considering that you are delivering "reliability" you might even consider that you need a Reliability Department to which maintenance is a subordinate activity. Integrated and collaborative approaches work best, yet traditional departmental boundaries still get in the way. What's needed is a shift of focus to the delivery of business results not departmental results. Many organizations today are struggling with this. They measure the wrong things and encourage the wrong behaviors.

Teamwork

There's an old saying that, "two heads are better than one." Teamwork has been proven time and again to produce superior results. It is the basis for many successful methods like RCM, PMO, RCFA, Total Productive Maintenance (TPM) and even the highly technical Evidence Based analytical methods. While your people are truly important both individually and collectively, it is organizations that make extensive use of teamwork, especially self-directed teams, that truly see exceptional performance. According to organizational guru, Margaret Wheatley[4], self-organized teams bring out the best in people and those teams will be far more productive. They encourage creativity, participation, innovation. They use team / peer pressure (ever so subtly) to ensure that people are all working towards the same goals. In turn, these teams deliver enhanced productivity and superior results.

When we work with our customers to implement change across organizations of any size, we use a project charter to define how teams will be structured and how they will interact. Team leaders are members of steering teams or steering committees depending on their roles. They are not representatives of their teams to the senior level, they are there to lead in the direction that the leadership team has set. Direction flows down. Reporting and all it implies flows up.

Smaller teams tend to be more effective than larger teams, provided they have sufficient breadth and depth of knowledge to handle assigned tasks. When teams grow into large groups or departments, they begin to need more formal management structures and processes in order to remain effective. Malcolm Gladwell[5] explains that if you have a group with more than 150 people, you will find formalized approaches necessary. In groups with fewer than 150 people such as a small manufacturing plant, a degree of informality often works well.

Keep this in mind when looking at organizational arrangements. Smaller groups and less formal organizations do not need or rely on "command and control" to get things done – management becomes easier. Command and control methods often stifle

---

[4] "Finding Our Way – Leadership in Uncertain Times", Margaret Wheatley, 2005, Beckett-Koehler Publishers, San Francisco

[5] "The Tipping Point – How Little Things Can Make A Big Difference", Malcolm Gladwell, 2000, Abacus, Great Britain

initiative and creativity and harms productivity, especially in to-day's well educated, socially aware and tech savvy work force. I like to consider managers and leaders to be supporters for their teams – they shouldn't need to control, but they definitely need to nurture. Command and control styles are giving way to "command and nurture".

Assembly Line Management Systems

This topic probably belongs in books on business, not a book on physical assets, yet it is entirely relevant. I hope that executives who read this will give this a lot of thought.

Let's look at the military. It is structured with distinct levels and ranks and having very well defined boundaries between groups that specialize in different activities and environments: army, navy, air force, artillery, infantry, armor, bombing, fighters, patrol, etc. For much of the time they work independently of each other and do not need to rely on one another very much, if at all. They do a lot of training – in fact, most of their time is spent in training although not in classrooms as those of us in industry probably envision. However, when they need to work together against a common threat (enemy) they come together and support each other very well, or at least to the limits of their capabilities, up to and including dying in the process. Command and control and teamwork are not mutually exclusive.

Most businesses are structured like the military with different groups and levels: executives, managers, supervisors, workers, finance, human resources, operations, production, accounting, maintenance, engineering, projects, etc. Most of the time (in fact almost all the time) they work independently of each other because they do not need each other most of the time – or so they think. Unlike the military that battles a common threat only occasionally (think of it as a business challenge), they are battling it all the time without break. However, they rarely work together to achieve their shared goals – profitability, service delivery, safe operations, etc. In fact, most of them actually work at cross purposes.

Their goals are departmental, not organizational in nature. Command and control is practiced but teamwork isn't.

A few organizations have teamwork figured out – at least at the plant and operational levels. Toyota with its famous Toyota Production System is perhaps the best example. Yet Toyota's divisions don't necessarily work well together. Recently was replacing a car that was damaged in an accident. The dealership had our new car within a week of the accident – we had sent a deposit. The rest of the transaction timing was dependent on the insurance company and Toyota's own financing division. Insurance was covering it all, they processed their paperwork and sent checks to Toyota's financing division in reasonable time considering the time of year (early winter) and number of accident claims they were flooded with. The financing became a major hold up. Even with money in hand from the insurer, they couldn't process paperwork in any sort of timely manner. The whole process took about 6 weeks from accident to new car in the garage and much of that time was hold ups in processing paper in Toyota's own finance division. Why?

Companies are structured like the military from top to bottom, but they operate like assembly lines across functional departments and divisions. The assembly line is a wonderful invention that enables production of like products efficiently and quickly, value being added at each sequential step. It works well in a linear sequential manner. There's no doubt about what value is being added at each step. Businesses, like the military have functional demarcations that are supposed to add value and contribute to overall profitability, safety, etc. Like an assembly line value should be added with each function, but not with each step, so it doesn't end up working so well.

Functional areas, working in parallel with each other, are usually uncoordinated and lacing in common goals and incentives. They don't all work to achieve common goals. They work to achieve departmental (functional) goals and take it on faith that it will all come together to achieve corporate goals. Sadly that doesn't happen in many cases. Functional departments and divisions often work like they are completely independent of each other. They have their own goals and no overlapping responsibilities or accountability with other functional areas. It's like an assembly line with all steps operating in parallel and no coordination that results in a final product being put together.

It's beyond scope of this book to recommend a completely new way of structuring businesses. It is well within its scope however, to recommend far better coordination and cooperation. Managers won't usually do that on their own. They need leadership by someone who sees the bigger picture and values the contributions that each of those functional components can add, if they work together. That leader will probably be somewhat visionary and will likely need help to keep that alive. Governance systems that reinforce the bigger picture approach to managing the business are going to be needed. Performance metrics, compensation and reward schemes will be needed to reinforce that collaborative approach and nudge it in the direction of becoming corporate culture.

Learning and Development

Learning, training, and development are critical to companies that strive for excellence. Our educational systems are no longer geared towards industrial careers and the onus is shifting to companies to foster their own talent. Without a focus on developing people, companies will become victims of the demographic realities of our times. At the time of writing, the baby boom generation is half retired already, and much of the other half is marking time until retirement (which is near at hand for them). They have a great deal of knowledge and skill and in many cases the years of being told what to do, to check their brains at the door, that they are being paid for their time not their thinking, have demotivated them. Yet they do still care and want to leave a lasting legacy. Sadly, all too many organizations are failing to realize this and act to capture the wealth of knowledge and experience that has left or is about to "go out the door". Efforts to capture that are rewarded with the sustaining of successful and proven practices by your younger workers. Without that effort however, your organization is doomed to forget lessons learned and repeat the mistakes those older workers have already made.

Attracting, retaining and rewarding talent is critical. There is no point spending a great deal on recruiting and developing people in-house if you do not retain them through a competitive and attractive compensation program that recognizes their individual and team contributions and successes. The days of loyalty to companies and "careers for life" are long gone everywhere except in government. You need to keep your people engaged, challenged and motivated to stay. Encouraging career and personal development and then paying for new skills that get used at work are excellent ways to motivate and retain talent. If you think you will hold onto people because you pay "competitively", then think again. You are providing a revolving door for them to come and go.

Multi-skilling continues to grow in popularity as a means of developing workforce flexibility and enabling more efficient deployment of maintenance resources. It must however, be accompanied by suitable compensation to reward the effort put into attaining those additional skills, and you must use it. Like any muscle, if you don't use it, you will lose it.

In many industries where everyone has access to the same equipment, same processes, and same inputs, people may be the only sustainable competitive advantage.

Essentials

Essentials are those things that most people would recognize as maintenance activities. You will find these, to one degree or another, in every maintenance organization you visit. Lower performers probably know how to do these, but don't do them particularly well. They don't stand a chance with anything more advanced if they want to choose excellence. Higher performers are well positioned to excel. You want to do them well in order have a stable operation with costs under control, even if not yet optimized. The Essentials will help your maintenance organization to be efficient, have high levels of "wrench time", minimize avoidable delays in work being done, no excuses for work being only partially done and no work being done more than once. It's done the right way the first time and on time. With the Essentials you can save a great deal of your maintenance costs, but it can take time to realize the benefits because these many parts must work well together.

Work Management

Essentials are the activities, processes and tools you use to deliver the most visible aspect of Maintenance – people working in the field efficiently, with precision and obtaining visible results – operating equipment. The most basic process in maintenance is "work management" – getting your maintainers active in the field doing work on your systems. With skilled trades who care, you will be benefiting from precision maintenance practices. Fasteners, lubrication, alignments and balancing will get a lot of attention. Your work management process must be supported by a reliable source of parts and materials. The work you do must cover compliance to regulations, some basic care activities by operators and some form of proactive maintenance program. Your department is most likely managed using some performance indicators and those are fed with data gathered and stored in a computerized maintenance management system to support deci-sion making. Do these well, and you will have a controlled and stable base for reliability improvements and choosing excellence. Do them poorly and your maintenance will tend to be reactive and chaotic.

"Failing to plan is planning to fail," Benjamin Franklin.

Planning is a key foundational part of good work manage-ment. At the core of the maintenance function is work management: a six-step process for getting maintenance work done: identify, plan, schedule, assign, execute and learn as de-picted below. You want to minimize the amount of work that follows the red line – unplanned, unscheduled and reactive.

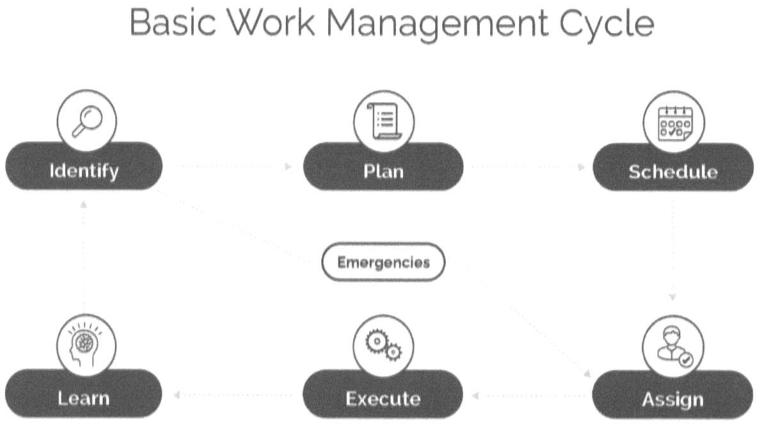

Basic Work Management Cycle

Figure 5 Work Management Process

Without a defined process of managing the work and your workforce, their deployment becomes reactive to emergencies, timed by breakdowns (not you), and your maintenance costs will be high – much higher than they need to be. Work done in those reactive situations is anywhere from 1.5 to 3 times as expensive fully planned work that is carried out to a schedule. In some oper-ational environments the direct costs of being reactive can be very high and the opportunity costs even higher. Bear in mind that not all of the costs associated with being reactive are captured in one maintenance budget account. The cost of emergency work are usually much higher that the costs you record in your accounting systems – consider lost production, fines, demurrage, expedited shipping, premium pricing on last minute part orders, and other "penalties" when your equipment fails. Often the most severe outcome is loss of reputation, resulting in loss of customers and Revenue from them. If your business suffers a lot of that, your insurers will see it as increased risks and your premiums will be higher. If your bankers see it, they may be less favorably inclined to help finance your business potentially causing cash flow problems. Choosing excellence requires a mastering the work management process. Sadly however, far too few companies really do master it.

The simple six step work management cycle is something that highly effective maintenance departments do well. Scheduling, using nothing more than reasonable estimates of job duration and a rudimentary check to make sure materials are available is a great first step to enhanced productivity. There is little reason to start a job, if you cannot finish it and parts unavailability is one of the biggest challenges resulting from poor or no planning. Over time, more thorough planning will enhance the gains. Not only will work be less expensive to execute, good work management will free up craftsperson time to do more work and have the work done when it is required. Identification of needed parts and materials with plenty of lead time helps Maintenance stores to have what you need on hand, when you need it. Individual tradesperson / artisan productivity can nearly double. This improved efficiency opens the door to enhanced effectiveness through a variety of reliability improvement initiatives. It can also be used to reduce overtime and use of contractors by bringing work in house.

There are planning and budgeting cycles to consider. These range from detailed job plans through project, shutdown, and annual cycles, to strategic multiyear and asset life-cycle focus. The basics of planning and scheduling apply to all work. Individual jobs, projects, and shutdowns are all managed the same way, the only difference being scale and scope of work. Shutdowns in particular are high-cost, intensive activities that require the Operations to shutdown, resulting in zero revenue generation. It is important to get it right and avoid the temptations to do too much unplanned or poorly planned work in the available time windows. Good use of predictive maintenance techniques helps identify work scope and reduces the volume of work arising during shutdowns.

As you might expect, mobile workforce management differs from fixed plant management. Communications are challenging and a variety of technologies have been developed to deal with that. Work order and work reporting via tablets, laptop computers, smart phones and other ruggedized hand held devices is becoming common in mobile work environments and even in larger plants. Systems deployed in the cloud are great enablers provided connectivity and bandwidth are not issues.

Scheduling plays a big role in efficiency because of the need for travel from job to job. Technologies like Global Positioning Systems coupled with Geographic Information Systems help keep mobile workforces productive while meeting the demands of far-flung customers and assets. Mobile work crews are autonomous by nature and carry much of their own support parts and materials with them, but those must be replenished regularly or excessive travel time will result. Planning and scheduling to accommodate geographic considerations is a key to success in managing a mobile workforce.

Work management is the most important maintenance process. Paying attention to it provides substantial benefits. Effective planned and scheduled work is more efficient and less expensive than planned and unscheduled work, and even less expensive than unplanned work. It is enabled by good integration of work management and MRO materials processes and operators doing their part in "Basic Care".

Basic Care

We've heard about people who rent cars then drive it like they stole it. They don't own it and consequently don't really care about it so long as it does what they need and while they need it. The corollary to that is the care we put into our own cars. We own them, depend on them, trust them to be safe for our loved ones, and so we care for them. Basic care is a lot like what the car owner does, when he cares for his own car.

It has been said that there is no point doing work right, if you do the wrong work – good point. But just what constitutes the "right work". There are advanced methods for determining optimum proactive maintenance programs, but without a reasonable foundation in the Essentials, those efforts can be wasted. Basic Care is about doing the work that just makes sense and without a lot of in-depth analysis. Getting the minimum done to comply with regulatory requirements and keep out of trouble is a part of it (most companies do that well), but it is not enough.

Doing basic maintenance activities well can make a big difference.

Parts, assemblies and equipment are all held together with various fasteners that must be strong enough to do the job. They often have specified torque requirements to ensure proper loading – pay attention to those. Over and under-tightening are both problematic. Lubrication in the form of the right grease, oil and hydraulic fluids, kept clean, free of contaminants and dry is the life blood of all mechanical equipment. Lubrication failures of one sort or another can be a big contributor to plant downtime. Proper attention to lubrication and lubricants is essential. When rotating equipment are coupled together, like a pump and its motor, they run longer, with less stress and consume less power if they are properly and precisely aligned. Anything that rotates at speed can create vibrations. If bad enough, those can damage the rotating equipment or even equipment nearby. Precision balancing, ensuring smooth operation is another often overlooked step in repairs.

Make sure that all your proactive maintenance efforts are fit for purpose. Following manufacturers' recommendations is not necessarily the best approach and strict compliance to them could cost you more than necessary. What's worse, that work can sometimes even induce failures. Putting a PM program in place quickly will be beneficial. If you don't have such a program, then get a copy of "Uptime" and use its Appendix C as a guideline to get yourself started. Use your experience with your assets to adjust those recommended actions to suit. If you already have a basic PM program, then you should be realizing some benefit of being proactive. You can always return to it later and refine it using PM Optimization or RCM.

Another important basic care activity is enterprise housekeeping – not just to keep things looking neat and tidy, but to eliminate waste and contamination. If things like tools and parts are easier to find and in good condition when you need them, you save yourself effort. If there's less dirt, there's less contaminant around to get into and damage the equipment, and it becomes easier to troubleshoot. It's also a nicer place to work and happier workers tend to work better.

5S is a well-proven approach to creating a highly productive work environment for maintainers, operators and even office workers. Borrowed from the world of Total Productive Maintenance (TPM) and the Toyota Production System, but applicable in any environment, the 5S pillars – Sort, Set-in-Order, Shine, Standardize and Sustain condition will simplify, condition and make your workplace far more effective while helping to eliminate a variety of wasteful practices and old habits.

Implementing basic care is one of the first steps in getting an out-of-control work environment under control and functioning both effectively and efficiently. In fact, the act of implementing it helps to foster a greater sense of ownership in your workforce which in turn leads to a greater motivation to keep things working well. When implemented in parallel with planning and scheduling you can realize some amazing gains in your workforce productivity.

Taking basic care all the way to "lean" can produce amazing benefits. Documented benefits from a full "lean" environment include: 75% less inventory and work in process, quality improvements of 40%, worker efficiency increased by up to 50%, lead time reductions of up to 50%, overall equipment effectiveness increases of up to 25%, and customer satisfaction improves by 75%.

MRO Materials Management

Perhaps the most blamed, and least well understood, cause of delays in getting repairs done is parts. Arguably the provision of parts is not even a maintenance responsibility, but that wouldn't be entirely accurate. Of course most parts related problems arise from a lack of integration of maintenance planning and the various supply chain processes aimed at providing those parts when needed and in the correct quantities. Here we deal with making sure your maintainers have what they need and when they need it.

Maintenance, repair and overhaul (MRO) materials are needed for most maintenance jobs. The thousands of parts that make up your MRO stores are all materials that do not go into the finished product. They are accounted for as indirect costs and go into the equipment and systems you use to produce. Usually, they are managed by the same supply chain organization that manages production materials, but they must be managed quite differently. Unlike the usually limited range of production raw materials that come in large quantities, MRO comprises thousands of parts and items often ordered in small quantities. They can however, make up the bulk of your purchasing department work simply because there are so many of them. They are not usually managed by the reliability and maintenance group, and it's usually good that they are not, but they are absolutely essential to its success.

Without the right spare parts and materials many maintenance jobs simply cannot be done. There is little point planning and scheduling work, if you cannot rely on a dependable supply of the needed parts when you need them. In many under-performing organizations, you'll actually hear a great deal of complaining about parts unavailability and slow procurement, especially in emergencies. In truth, that reflects badly on work planning more than materials management, yet both must share the blame. If you want excellence in maintenance, you also need excellence in materials management. Your work management and materials management processes must be integrated closely, and work together as if they were one seamless process, or you cannot achieve all the benefits that work management can deliver.

In teaching "Uptime", I use a simple but effective exercise to illustrate the importance of planning and scheduling. There are three teams, each has a box of toy blocks to build identical models. One team has all the parts and all the instructions, another has all the instructions but a few parts are missing, and the third team has no instructions and a few parts are missing. The first team always finishes first by quite a margin. Then, taking twice to three times as long, the second team will finish. The third team usually doesn't finish and by the time they've given up they've stolen parts off the "sample" model at the front of the room and begged the other teams to share their instruction sheets. Plans are important. Parts are important. Skills also matter and experience playing with your children actually helps here, but it is plans and parts that really make the difference. They are both needed to execute effectively!

Top performing operations rarely need to delay or halt work because of unavailable parts. That happens as a result of the work management processes failing to communicate material requirements to the supply chain in a timely manner. Excellent plans with very precise identification of materials are of little use, if they are communicated without sufficient lead time to account for supplier lead times and delivery. It can also be a result of failures of the supply chain to deliver on time, provided they had the advance notice they needed. Lead times for materials are a major consideration too, but if the processes you use are well thought through, then lead times become manageable. In fact, if your communication from maintenance planning right through the supply chain is very good, lead times can be reduced.

Availability of spares is important, especially for critical and items with longer lead times. MRO materials usually make up a small portion of most companies' material inventories and spending, but the bulk of the inventory transactions resulting from the large number and timing of different parts required. These parts and materials usually represent a small portion of your inventory investment, but they can be critical to running your plant. Individual parts can be of any value, they are purchased and used in small quantities, they are often slow moving and they can be difficult to source (especially if you are in an aging facility), yet they are essential to getting planned work done as planned and on schedule. Managing MRO materials is a big and very important job. If MRO materials processes are not improved in lock step with maintenance, your ability to deliver Uptime will be seriously limited.

The more proactive your maintenance work becomes, the more predictable material demands will be. Decisions to stock or rely on just-in-time supply based on lead times and known demands can be made with confidence. For spares that may have a big impact on machine availability, risk based calculations are best suited to determining sparing levels. Those risk based calculations are often completely foreign to MRO materials managers who typically don't have the engineering and statistics background required. In our work on MRO inventory, we use a fairly sophisticated spares and inventory modelling tool that requires engineering inputs. Without such a tool, most inventory managers will struggle with decisions about which of their slow moving items really should be kept, and which should be discarded. Very slow moving items that may be high value when needed, are at risk of being discarded because of their low usage. I refer to those as "insurance" spares, but the value of that insurance is often not understood by MRO stores personnel.

All too often they rely solely on calculations used in retail supply (e.g.: re-order points, economic order quantities, min / max inventory levels, etc.). Those work well for those fast moving, low value, short lead time items, but not so well for MRO inventory that, if missing, can keep your operation shutdown. Those calculations simply don't account for risk of stock-out or unavailability of supported plant. In retail, items move fast or they won't be stocked for sale. If they stock-out, you risk losing a sale, but you don't shut down the store.

Some MRO material moves quickly – fasteners, seals, gaskets, smaller bearings, electrical devices, pipe fittings, etc. But there is much more that is specific to one or two pieces of equipment that don't fail all that often. Demand for those will be low. Indeed, for that MRO material you very likely won't have the history of demand and turnover that will give you comfort that stock levels are correct using those simpler calculations.

Your MRO stores is, by the nature of what you store and manage, more sophisticated, higher value and has a potentially big business impact. It requires deeper thinking than you find in most retail operations. It warrants somewhat more sophisticated approaches to managing the quantities and indeed the quality of the inventory holdings. Unlike retail items in a store, some MRO material must also be maintained while in stores. Some has a shelf life – like elastomers and gasket materials. Some electronic devices may need to be powered-up in storage. Large rotating elements, like electric motors or compressor rotors may need to be turned to avoid bearing damage and sagging of the rotating element between its bearings. Some items require careful control of humidity and temperature.

In figure 6 (following) you can see how different maintenance approaches lead to differences in demand and therefore the type of calculation needed to "right size" your stores item holdings.

Proactive maintenance is always carried out at fixed intervals so demand is very precisely forecast. Condition based maintenance often requires no material itself, but occasionally will identify incipient failures that if left uncorrected will become much worse. You get some warning for those and potentially even enough to rely on supply only when they arise. If there are some long lead items involved however, you can at least forecast demand based on historic failure rates.

Reactive work, that typically can't be addressed proactive, or isn't worth addressing proactively will also occur, but there should be less of it. You will probably need spares for that but again, historic failure history should be a useful gauge of demand.

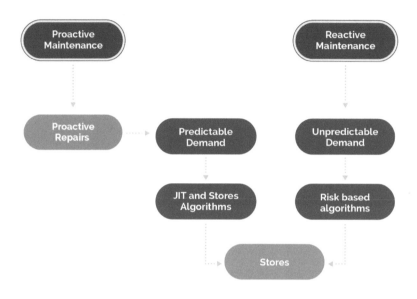

Figure 6 Proactive is far more manageable

Taking advantage of that requires that information flows between maintenance and MRO supply management groups. Communications between work management (specifically planning) and MRO Material processes are key success factors. Integrating materials management processes such as stores issues and returns, receiving notifications, and purchasing with the maintenance planning and scheduling parts of the work management process must happen. Figure 7, below shows (notionally) how that should occur – both processes use the same bill of materials, planning specifies what's needed, MRO obtains it, tells scheduling know when it is available, execution consumes it and sometimes generates repairables that must also be managed.

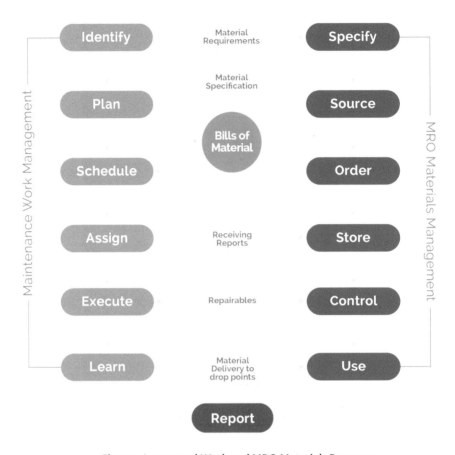

Figure 7 Integrated Work and MRO Materials Processes

There is no point ordering materials for a rush job if the parts arrive only to sit on a shelf because maintenance doesn't know they have arrived. This becomes even worse if the job is urgent and maintenance works outside the normal procurement processes to secure the parts themselves and ends up double-ordering (one order by stores and one by maintenance) to meet production demands.

Such "out of process" direct purchasing activity usually results in the growth of "shadow inventories" and undermines good materials management practice. It becomes increasingly difficult for MRO materials managers to forecast maintenance needs if the material requirements do not flow through the channels that collect usage data to forecast demand.

The maintenance parts (MRO) storeroom can be a sore point for your maintainers if it and its processes are not managed well and integrated with work management. There is much that can be done to make it efficient and cost effective. Keep in mind that if you are experiencing trouble in this area today you probably need to work on both your work management and materials management processes together. Until you get both of those sorted out, clear up the unofficial stores of shadow inventory (parts in the maintainers lockers and desks, under benches, etc.), you are better off to hold what may seem like excessive inventory than to incur the high cost of extra downtime while you wait for parts to repair critical equipment. Avoid the temptation to clean up stores on its own, without changing the situation. That is often a penny-wise and pound foolish approach, as the problems are likely to return. The key to success here is to have maintenance, inventory, and supply chain management all working together.

While correcting MRO materials problems can save money in the form of less working capital, fewer repair delays, and lower logistics costs, correcting those problems without also correcting the other Essentials can be a waste of effort. In fact, until you have work management processes working well so that schedule compliance is no longer an issue, you might even benefit from having too much inventory of MRO Materials. Those extra parts on the shelves in your storeroom are indeed tying up working capital, but the amount they tie up is usually far less than the opportunity cost of lost revenue from production downtime while waiting for parts. Timing of improvements in MRO Materials should be tied in with improvements in work management.

Performance Management

"What gets measured, gets managed", the proverb is often attributed to William Thomson, Lord Kelvin, a Scottish physicist in the 1880's.

If you are going to manage effectively and influence behavior to achieve higher performance, then an Essential tool is the measurement and use of key performance indicators. Performance management is needed for good maintenance management. Costs are important, results are important, and so are the processes you use to turn costs into beneficial results, but put the focus where it needs to be most – on the processes. Keep an input → process → output model in mind. While you may want high reliability (an output) at low cost (an input) you can only get there by improving the processes that turn that money into results. Performance management is central to seeing problems with processes and activities, then managing those in order to deliver greater cost effectiveness. Striving for low cost alone, is a dangerous game to play – you simply can't manage cost directly, as costs are an outcome of what you do. Cut spending in the wrong area and you increase it more elsewhere. You don't want to play whack-a-mole with your spending – target what matters – your processes. Have a look back at Figure 1 – the major processes you want to control and manage are shown. Each has several measures of performance that can be monitored and used to gauge and guide improvements. The output is at the top - $/unit output.

Good maintenance is about sustaining performance, not repairing what is already broken. I've often thought that we should have "Reliability" departments, not "Maintenance" departments. Put the emphasis on what matters – reliability – the output. When you are experiencing fewer breakdowns and repairs, it's a sign that maintenance is working well. It is not a signal to cut proactive maintenance costs. That proactive spending is entirely discretionary, but absolutely essential to the results you want to achieve – lower costs, and higher output and revenue.

Being effective in managing maintenance performance entails management of a number of measures that tell you about the work management process, materials management, training, tradespeople, reliability improvement efforts, and so on. What you measure, how you measure, and how often you measure are all important. Having realistic process performance metrics and targets for performance helps, but beware of the gaming that can occur to make things look good. If low performance numbers are used to reflect on individuals' performance they can almost always be made to look good. Focus upon improving the performance, NOT upon improving the measurement numbers. Measuring the wrong things, fudging the numbers and twisting definitions of what is measured all to meet arbitrary performance goals are all ways of fooling yourself into thinking you are doing better than you really are. Using the wrong or only single measures can result in unexpected and often wrong behaviors that generate unintended outcomes of sometimes surprising and very negative results.

Benchmarking has its place in helping you set realistic and achievable performance targets as well as learning about the practices that high performers use to achieve their performance. When talking about benchmarks, make it clear whether you are talking about numbers and targets, or good practices. Both can be benchmarked. Be wary of anyone who refers to benchmark numbers often – there simply aren't a lot out there that are widely available and care is needed to interpret those that are.

You want to emulate successful practices and set realistic measurable objectives for your organization. Setting an unrealistic target can also lead to some odd behaviors as those being measured or managing the measures, strive to meet those targets.

Ensure measures are within the control of those being measured. Otherwise, it results in a cynical situation of benefiting when they do not deserve it, and being "punished" also when they do not deserve it.

A number of widely used numeric benchmark standards are available for use if all you want is hard targets. You don't need an expensive benchmarking project to set targets. Benchmarking visits to see how others work however, can be very helpful, but focus on what they do, and how they achieved it, more than the numbers. If you don't have the budget for those extensive studies though, you can always fall back on experience consultants who have been around and seen both good and bad practices. Knowing what doesn't work, can often be just as valuable as knowing what does.

Balanced score cards provide an approach to tracking performance measures so that you achieve a balance between (or among) competing priorities. Tradeoffs are inevitable and a classic example of this the trade-off between inventory cost reduction and maintenance service levels. Watching a balanced set of measures that also considers the uptime outputs, empowers you to make informed decisions that optimize performance in all areas to achieve the desired business output.

One customer, a large postal operation, used a single measure of performance for its maintenance managers – downtime. If any letter sorting machine had a failure resulting in downtime of more than 30 minutes it was reported nationally and showed up on a monthly summary report. To avoid the embarrassment of having their names published nationally, the maintenance managers improved "downtime" performance by making repairs more rapidly. To achieve that they had stores of just about every possible part stashed in cabinets beside each sorting machine. That resulted in a massive amount of parts inventory that didn't need to be there and tied up millions of dollars in working capital. Some balance would have helped!

Hoshin Kanri was mentioned earlier as a mechanism for strategy deployment. In addition to defining projects, activities and assigning responsibilities it also produces an array of key performance indicators that are used to mark both progress (of your improvements) and the results you generate. Performance indicators are an important link that ties the results you get from the processes you manage to the strategic goals you are working towards both within maintenance and asset management and at the corporate levels.

Performance measurement helps you keep track of where you are relative to where you want to go. Your strategy sets direction so you don't wander aimlessly. Measures keep you on the path by pointing out where correction is needed so that behavior can be modified accordingly. Well selected performance measures can help improve the overall financial measures.

Support Systems

Mike Currie, a good friend and colleague once said, "Software isn't strategy", and he went on to write a book about it. After years of helping organizations with new software it was evident that many of those organizations saw the software as a "solution", as if it could actually solve their problems! It can't and won't. A well thought out and well implemented software package can help make problem solving easier, but it won't solve your problems. It is just a tool and like any tool, its effectiveness is dependent upon the quality and suitability of the tool, and the capability of those wielding it. It must be the right tool for the job and used the right way, or you get disappointing results.

Computerized systems for management have become seemingly indispensable tools for just about any business. Remember the last power failure you experienced, and you will understand that there is very little that is not computerized these days – chances are that even your alarm clock stopped. Technology and application in business processes continues to grow and proliferate. Maintenance is a supporting business process. Its management can and does benefit from technology in a number of ways.

Most maintenance work is very hands' on, requiring parts and step-by-step procedures – it is not computerized. The work can be complex and there is a lot to be managed for each job, as well as many jobs to manage. Doing so efficiently today requires fairly sophisticated tools. Using those tools effectively will improve the efficiency with which you deliver maintenance services. Use them poorly (as sadly many do) and you only add cost while distracting, rather than informing yourself with data.

There are two broad categories of technology that maintainers work with: support (analytical) systems and management information systems. The first category includes the various specialized support systems for data gathering, processing, analysis, and decision-making support. The MRO spares modelling software we use is an example.

These tools are meant to help today's knowledge workers, your maintenance technicians and engineers, do their jobs efficiently and effectively. They are used to monitor equipment condition, analyze equipment performance trends, analyze failure history data, perform complex reliability calculations, provide support to equipment replacement decisions, forecast probabilities, assist or control laser alignment and balancing. They are often designed as stand-alone systems to be used by trained specialists. These tools, in the right hands, can produce remarkable results and quickly earn a return on your investment. They are usually not designed, nor well suited, to integrate seamlessly with management information systems which are typically for tracking transactions.

A big mistake sometimes made is to attempt to integrate those analytical support systems with your business management systems. Attempts to do so can be costly and eventually they will prove to be fruitless. One customer attempted to integrate their

Reliability Centered Maintenance analysis software with their EAM. They spent hundreds of thousands of dollars over many months to no avail. A system that is based on failure modes couldn't easily and simply integrate with one based on work orders that may or may not be tied to failure modes, making the investment in integration questionable.

The second category of technologies includes the various management information systems: computerized maintenance management systems (CMMS), enterprise asset management (EAM) systems, and enterprise resource planning (ERP) systems. These systems automate business processes and information flows associated with a variety of business transactions within and supporting maintenance.

These systems use the work order as their primary transaction document. They can produce management reports, schedules, and graphs from which it is possible to see trends in performance measures and then make management decisions. Their main function is to support management processes and decision making. They might reside on your own servers or in a cloud based service. They can be very expensive to acquire, install, implement, and operate. They can take months or even years to get going. However, when coupled with business process redesign, the implementation of effective maintenance, inventory, and supply chain processes, they can add a great deal of value. To get that value, it does require that you ensure you are working effectively, and that may require you to optimize your reliability and maintenance processes. There is insufficient payback to justify a system if only automating transactional processes, aka "paving the cow path".

All of these systems are undergoing constant development and expansion of their capability. One colleague jokes that whenever an IT provider loses a competitive bid process because of some peculiar functionality they may be missing, then it gets added in the next release. The result is many of these systems have extensive arrays of capabilities, much of which most users do not need.

The single purpose and simpler forms of management systems tend to be easier to use. They are designed for maintenance and sometimes even pre-developed configurations for a specific industry. They are tailored to how the industry works and they can be very simple to use. Other systems are designed for use in broader ranges of industries and may include more business functions that are not even related to maintenance. As a rule, the broader the capability and the greater the functionality of a system, the more difficult it is to use.

User friendliness is of critical importance if you are going to get value from your computer systems. If they aren't used by your employees because it is too difficult, they will deliver no value and simply become a money sink, and a source of frustration to those who are expected to enter information and those who want to use the information that was to be provided. Of course suppliers of these systems are working hard to change that, but they can only do so much with software. A lot of the problem is behavioral. One development is the emergence of standards for data interchange using internet architectures that would permit multiple systems, each having different purposes, to share data. This opens up the possibility for specialized decision support systems to gather needed data from management systems and vice versa.

IIoT, AI and ML

Today we hear a lot about the industrial internet of things (IIoT), Artificial Intelligence (AI) and Machine Learning (ML). They technologies continue the evolution of computerized technology with the intention of making our life easier.

So far, the IIoT is a really a new way of deploying technologies that already exist. Instead of having hard-wired sensors that record various signals and send them to an analyzer to tell us whether or not the equipment being monitored is in good condition, the IIoT deploys sensors wirelessly, in larger numbers and with more computing capability on or near the sensor itself. That "edge" computing keeps bandwidth and centralized computing requirements for analyzing signals down. The IIoT greatly expands the potential for Predictive Maintenance, specifically online condition monitoring to give us early warning of failures that are developing but not yet fully progressed to loss of function. In concept, the IIoT will deploy vast numbers of sensors, each at low cost and connected wirelessly (via Bluetooth or Wifi) to systems that will give us warnings, alarms and trigger actions such as emergency shutdowns.

We see the IIoT in mines where telemetry is used to monitor and in some cases drive and operate mobile equipment. We see it in cars equipped with emergency beacons and safety systems that trigger live help in the event that an accident incapacitates the driver. We see it in smart home systems and smart buildings.

The IIoT has tremendous potential in industrial applications. I do have one concern – are we ready for it? In control rooms if you find alarms and warnings that are being silenced and ignored, you have to ask if we don't already have too much information. The right information at the right time is very helpful, but too much, constantly or at the wrong time, can be distracting.

Artificial intelligence and machine learning go together. Machines (computers really) are able to learn from the experience of what happens when decisions are made on the basis of information that is presented. This "feeds" the artificial brain (the computer) and it then learns. Machines can learn by programming rules that are then followed (if this, then that, etc.) or they can learn by observing patterns in the data they receive. Computers can learn games rapidly and become masters of those games in amazingly short time frames. Such capabilities are driving marketing campaigns, observing your activities on line so that you can be presented with advertisements the computer deems to be of interest to you. What you do, is being watched very closely, it determines what will be presented to you, and all in the hope of influencing your buying behavior.

That same sort of technology can be used to make decisions in industrial systems. Of particular interest is the use of this technology in conjunction with condition monitoring data and equipment health monitoring. Even operational control data, used to set various actuators in response to what is happening in a production process, can be used as indictor of equipment health. Those signals must be interpreted and correlated to "unhealthy" states in the equipment. When production stops unexpectedly, it is fair to assume that something has failed. Eventually the algorithms will be able to predict when this is likely to occur. But stoppages could also be for other reasons. The AI needs to recognize those and learn them also.

Traditional condition monitoring is used to forecast when equipment will fail due to mechanical or other causes that tend to occur randomly. It is intended to give warnings so we can act in a timely manner and avoid failure consequences. The condition signals are usually streams of good data, but the corresponding failure event data, often held in maintenance management systems, is often flawed.

At the time of writing, the machine learning and AI algorithms need good data. The CMMS and EAM systems that abound today are often populated with data that isn't quite fit for purpose. Caution is needed in using those, at least until the point in time when we can rely on the data in those maintenance systems to be accurate, complete and fit for its purpose. Today, there is still much work to be done on that front.

The world of maintenance support and management systems is complex and crowded with competing products. Explore what you really need to achieve, define your processes and how you want the systems to help, keep the choices as simple as you can. In the realm of IT, a large and long term investment will be difficult to recover – no matter which software you use, you can count on it changing soon. New releases and bug fixes will never stop!

Choosing Excellence

This is where we can find the real money. Maintenance costs tend to be a big focus, yet in fact they are but a portion of operating costs in most industries. By contrast, the value of pro-⟩ duction and revenue lost due to downtime can be huge. Those losses are typically far greater than the costs of maintaining the assets. Much of this book is about the maintenance the function (what we do), but what we really want is reliability – the result. Maintenance activities can be executed efficiently (the Essentials) but it's doing the right things that really matters. Choosing Excellence is about the effectiveness of our maintenance activities at delivering the needed availability.

Once you get the essentials right and working reasonably well, you are positioned to choose excellence. As in many sports, you must learn the basics, get practice, get good and keep on practicing to become excellent. In reliability and asset maintenance you need those essentials to be working reasonably well before your reliability efforts will be fully rewarded. While the essentials focus on doing the most basic work the right way, in this part we emphasize doing the right work. The biggest paybacks from maintenance are enables by achieving higher reliability. If your assets are reliable, then they can do what you want, when you want it and to the level of performance you want.

Reliability – being proactive

Doing the right maintenance is just as important as doing it the right way and in a timely manner. Physical assets have, by virtue of their design, an inherent level of reliability that they can attain. Let them degrade and that reliability suffers. Achieving that that reliability requires that you, operate the asset within its limits, and do the right maintenance. The right maintenance addresses the causes of the failures that can occur in that that particular design considering how it is operated. Equipment abuse or accidental damage can be a major cause of failures. We try to avoid that. The equipment must be operated within its technical limits and without abuse – again, something to be avoided. Don't overload it, don't expect more than its design provides for, and operate as intended. Assuming the asset is designed correctly to do what you want, then all that's left is the right maintenance.

Conceptually the old adage that an ounce of prevention is worth a pound of cure applies, but technically speaking, we don't just use preventive measures. Prevention implies that the failures be "preventable". That only happens if they occur with age or usage, not randomly. So our maintenance program must go beyond preventive measures.

The best maintenance sustains assets' productive capacity using what I call proactive measures – those actions that can be performed before we suffer the consequences of failures. We don't always prevent the failures, but we do aim at minimizing their consequences. With proactive maintenance, we avoid failures where possible and practical (prevent), forecast when failures that have begun will actually impact functionality (predict), and detect failed protective devices before we need them. Of course, in some cases those proactive actions may not be feasible or fully warranted. The cost of doing them may be greater than the cost of consequences. In those cases, we accept that our assets may sometimes be allowed to run to failure as the most appropriate option, depending upon failure consequences.

If we cannot use proactive measures, cannot tolerate failure (e.g.: perhaps the failure will result in fatalities or injuries), then we have little recourse but to redesign some aspect of the asset, how it is operated or how it fails to avoid those serious consequences. Redesign though, is often expensive and is used only as a last resort.

Risks and Consequences

Being proactive with your assets is all about managing the consequences of failures so they have the least negative impact on your business. Being proactive reduces risks. The advantage to doing this, is that major business impact due to equipment breakdown can be avoided. High performing companies manage proactively by foreseeing and avoiding problems. You can forecast what is likely to happen (failures) and decide in advance about what to do about those failures using a well-established and highly successful method – Reliability Centered Maintenance (RCM), compliant with standard SAE JA-1011. In its most recent form, RCM has been re-engineered and is now known as RCM-Re-engineered: RCM-R®.

The International Standards Organization (ISO) has produced standards on Asset Management: ISO 55000, 55001 and 55002. The word "risk" shows up often – managing assets is largely about managing risks. When you consider that many business operational, safety and environmental risks arise from failures of physical assets, their control and safety systems, you can begin to see why reliability becomes so important.

The world is very aware of risks and consequences. Major man-made and avoidable disasters keep occurring. Mine tailings dam failures, major electrical grid failures, commuter and freight train derailments, roadway overpass collapses, releases of natural gas, oil, and various other toxic substances into the environment, major fires due to poor containment combined with failures of protective devices and systems are all examples. The injuring and killing of employees and others as a result of equipment and systems failures, or from poor operating and maintenance practices are not uncommon. Most can actually be predicted and those risks managed with the methodologies that already exist, are proven to work well, and are widely available to us. So why do these disasters occur?

A recent tailings dam failure at a major mining operation in Brazil led to a major environmental catastrophe and over 250 fatalities. Higher than normal rains, poor drainage and brittle dam structure were blamed. The rain was the only factor that couldn't be controlled, but drainage could. The actual structure is very much a feature of the design. Like all failures, it occurred because of one or more three physical causes: inadequate design, inadequate operational practices, and/or inadequate maintenance. All three are likely factors in the case of that dam. Investigations reached a point sufficient for regulatory authorities in Brazil to charge a former CEO along with a total of 15 senior people in his company and an engineering firm with some serious criminal offences. You don't want to be in their shoes.

You may think that your industry can't create such disasters. Yet mining isn't unique in its ability to be harmful. A number of food manufacturers have sickened and killed customers with tainted product. Processing plants have injured and killed workers and by-standers with fires and releases that were supposed to be dealt with automatically by protective devices and systems that failed to operate. Trains have derailed due to excessive speeding on corners, because of wheel bearing failures and because of brake failures when the train was stationary on an inclined siding. This list is long. Think of the potential in your industry and realize that even one injury or fatality is probably enough to earn you a lot of unwanted attention. Moreover, you will want to live comfortably with yourself, knowing that you've done all you can to avoid harm for yourself, your employees, your customers, and the public in general, and the environment.

My point to you is that society is becoming far less tolerant of those who are responsible for the organizations that cause harm. Standards have arisen because it is such a wide-spread problem that needs to be addressed. Regulations are become more numerous (and sadly not always well informed) as a legalistic knee-jerk reaction to events that may be repeated due to our collective failure to use what we know and have available to us, to do the right things. We need to do the right things or we'll become so tied up in regulations and legal proceedings that we won't be able to do the jobs that our companies thought they hired us for.

Doing the Right Things

RCM was developed in the aircraft industry and has achieve significant reliability improvements in aircraft. It is more than 120 times safer to fly today than it was before RCM was developed. Despite its aeronautical roots, today RCM can be used in any industry and on any type of physical asset. When developing a maintenance program from scratch for a new project, it is unbeatable.

RCM includes a logical 7 step process (sub-processes 3 to 7 in figure 8). It can be applied to any asset in the early design stages, in the detailed design stages (preferably both) or later, after the asset has entered service.

RCM leverages the results of extensive studies of how things fail, combined with an understanding of the consequences of those failures to prompt logical decision making on asset failure management policies, failure mode by failure mode. It produces maintenance tasks (preventive, predictive and detective), operator tasks (e.g. very specific inspection rounds), decisions to run to failure (where consequences are tolerable), and decisions to make modifications to procedures, processes, design and other factors that may be leading to failures or reduce the consequences of those failures.

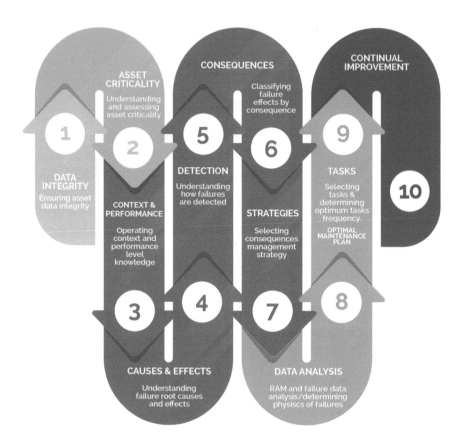

Figure 8 RCM-R - enahnced and SAE JA-1011 compliant

One of the great strengths of RCM is that it does not require failures to have occurred in order to perform the analysis. You only need to know that a failure could occur and its likelihood. This can be done from the knowledge and experience with the failure of components and assemblies that make up the assets, or from experience with similar assets. By forecasting what could happen and putting a failure consequence management strategy in place, we are being proactive in managing failure consequences to our business.

Trained RCM analysis teams, led by a highly-qualified Facilitators, anticipate the most likely failure modes, and then deals with them and their consequences before the fact. Above all, RCM offers high reliability at optimum cost. You don't want cheap maintenance or expensive maintenance, you want the right amount of the right maintenance. RCM balances costs with risks in order to meet what your organization deems tolerable. Safety, environmental performance, quality, productivity of your assets and maintenance costs all improve. It is always applied specifically for your assets in your operating environment. Any tendency to over- or under-maintain, often a result of using other methods or following manufacturers' recommendations, is avoided.

Since its development in the 1970's RCM has been used extensively in aircraft, avionics, nuclear power, military systems, various fleet management environments, mining, ore-processing, oil and gas extraction, refining, chemicals, pulp and paper, gas, water, waste water and electric utilities, telecoms, pharmaceuticals, facilities management, automated plants, and even hospitals. Today, you can find it in use in all sorts of capital-intensive industries where sustainable reliability is important. It is the cornerstone of many reliability improvement program especially those in successful companies.

One customer, a large electrical distribution utility in a major city of over 2.5 million, used RCM to re-define their entire maintenance program for all of their 200 + installed asset classes.

We trained their analysis staff (engineers, technicians and field supervisors) in the analysis method. We selected 7 of them who met our criteria for becoming facilitators. Trained them and then carried out 8 pilot projects where they were mentored. Each project entailed analysis of a different class of troublesome assets. Across those 8 projects we averaged a 34% cost savings relative to the old, traditional maintenance program. For those 8 assets alone we identified $958,000 in maintenance program savings.

8/200
ASSETS

34%
SAVINGS
($958,000)

Figure 9 Pilot project savings on the first 8 of 200 assets

Reliability, as measured in the industry, also improved with gradual changes in their measurement of customer interruptions, and interruption durations. Our role in the project was over. Up to that point they had spent only $200,000 on our services and already paid for it almost 5 times over.

Those facilitators continued with the remainder of their assets. Over the next two years they obtained an average of just over 22% in maintenance budget savings, and improvements in reliability of many of those assets. The cost of the program was a tiny fraction of the savings overall. Those savings and the reliability improvements don't just occur once – they endure, ongoing for years to come.

The success of RCM is based on its sound technical underpinnings and depends heavily on careful application of the process and follow-up by implementing the resultant decisions. Because operational context can change over time, those results must be kept "fresh" in a continuous improvement cycle, as those changes to context occur.

The same electrical utility described above did indeed notice a change in operating context over a period of about 10 years. Proliferation of consumer electronics, vertical growth of the city which was constrained from outward growth (increasing its population density), and the introduction of time of use billing all conspired to add a heavier load spread more evenly over the entire 24 hour clock and that in turn changed how assets were failing. Adjustments to the original analyses were needed and carried out.

Critics of RCM and its various commercial variants are quick to point out that RCM is labor intensive, costly and prone to failure. Indeed it requires an investment of time on the part of a team. Most assets can be analyzed in less than a week, with complex assets requiring about 2 weeks. Many failures of well-run RCM analysis projects occurred because of a lack of follow through. The outputs of the analysis were not put into practice in the operational environment. If the operating context changes and the analysis and decisions are not updated an otherwise successful program can gradually degrade.

Successful organizations keep their RCM programs "alive" using reliability analysis (based on good data collection and experience in operating the assets) long after the initial analyses were carried out. In fact this aspect of reliability depends on good data collection and asset information management. Your IT systems can play a big role in maximizing the long-term return on your RCM investment.

Reliability – Continuous Improvement

RCM is not the only reliability improvement method you can use when choosing excellence. It will be the most rigorous approach, but it may also be overkill for some less critical equipment and systems. Using the right blend of reliability methods will be more cost effective and delivers just as good a result. For a Greenfield application you've got the time to use RCM, but if you are already in operation and have an "out of control" situation, then you may need quicker action. You need to reign in rampant failures quickly to gain control.

Equipment failures disrupt business. Once they have happened, you will want to avoid having them happen again. Some failures are a big deal and those acute situations can get a lot of attention. Fortunately most of those big failures don't happen often. Quite often, there are far less significant failures that are cumulatively very damaging. Because they are chronic and happen often and consume your resources when returning them to service, these failures are worth doing something about. Taming an out of control situation can be done using Root Cause Failure Analysis. RCFA can also be used as an enhancement to a program developed using RCM.

A few of our customers have use RCFA early in their Uptime implementation efforts to reduce the recurring failures that were draining resources on an all too frequent basis. By carefully examining the evidence around the failures, looking at what did and did not happen, they were able to identify likely causes of the failures and eliminate them. The frequency of failures was reduced to a far more manageable level. That freed up maintainers to spend more time on proactive maintenance that had been neglected, it had the desired effect, and reliability began to improve in other areas of their operations as well. Of course an important factor is their ability to execute whatever activities they determine to be necessary as a result of their RCFA. If they can't get those done, then the RCFA will have no impact.

There are several approaches to doing RCFA, the most simple being the "5 Whys" method. The table below shows a simple example of how the method works, beginning with an undesirable event and ending with identification of a problem that we can solve easily.

What happened?	Question
Pump stopped pumping	Why?
Motor tripped off line	Why?
Overloaded when pump impeller seized in pump housing	Why did the impeller seize?
It made contact with wearing rings when it experienced cavitation at the pump suction	Why did it have cavitation?
Operator mistakenly throttled flow to process using suction valve	Why did he make that mistake?

Answer
Operating instructions didn't specify to throttle only with the discharge valve

Table 1 Example of Five Whys Root Cause Analysis

With "5 Whys" you don't need to ask "why" 5 times every time you tackle a problem. You may get to a solution in fewer than 5 questions or it may take longer.

Other methods take different approaches and all require some form of evidence on which to base decisions. Regardless of which method you choose, RCFA is always only applied after failures have occurred. In that sense it is entirely reactive to those failures. It is a method of performing a sort of "post mortem" to determine what caused any particular failure, and developing solutions to prevent its reoccurrence. The intent is to eliminate the "root cause,"—an identifiable cause that you can manage in some practical way. RCFA targets known failures, usually the ones that have caused you the most "pain". Unfortunately, it is done after the fact, so you've already incurred the consequences of those failures at least once. However, because it is done on specific incidents, and there is likely evidence to aid decision making, it is very well targeted. It is highly effective and, in an out of control situation, it can deliver fantastic benefits quickly.

Despite it obvious advantages, keep in mind that developing your entire reliability program using RCFA would be foolish. RCM deals with those failures before they happen. If those failures have serious consequences you don't want to allow them to happen so doing something proactive to avoid that is advisable. After all, you wouldn't fly in a new aircraft if you knew they were developing the maintenance program using root cause methods!

Don't fool yourself into thinking you can use RCFA as a way of avoiding the effort and costs required to do RCM.

RCFA is also a very good way to enhance your RCM results. Even experienced analysis team can make mistakes and omissions, or the context could change, which eventually show up as failures that you were supposed to be preventing, predicting or detecting early. RCFA is a good way to analyze those failures and then apply the findings as enhancements to both the RCM analysis and in your ongoing failure management programs.

RCM requires a team effort. It's thorough and delivers excellent results but some organizations can't afford the time required for those teams to do their jobs. In those cases the application of RCM is usually limited only to the most critical systems. For lesser critical systems, Preventive Maintenance Review and Optimization (PMR/O) is used. It has two applications – one in cases where an existing PM program is in place that needs to be optimized (hence its name) and the other, where no PM program exists.

PMR/O uses an abridged RCM-derived logic to analyze, eliminate, or modify maintenance activities of existing programs by reverse engineering them. It attempts to identify failure modes that may have been missed by the original maintenance program. Although its approach is not as thorough as RCM, it has achieved some very good results and merits consideration for use with non-critical assets.

Decision optimization techniques and tools help maintainers (usually maintenance or reliability engineers) to make fact-based decisions or improve on decisions already made. RCM can be used before an asset is put into service or without good data about past failures. In those cases, decisions about task frequencies and failure modes are invariably subject to some degree of uncertainty. Once in service, some unanticipated failures may surface or the frequency of failures may not match original estimates. Optimization techniques are used to analyze the in-service data to validate or modify the original decisions. It is a form of data analysis that becomes more precise as failure data that can only be accumulated in service becomes available. These techniques can be very accurate provided the data they rely upon is accurate. Your IT support systems and their correct use become important reliability support tools, if they contain good data that is fit for purpose. If the data is flawed, or otherwise unfit for purpose, then there are knowledge elicitation techniques that can be deployed using interviews and carefully crafted questions.

Reliability enhancement requires good data. If RCM, RCFA and PM Optimization efforts lack good data inputs, then improvements using these methods later will require improvements to data collection and management. Many CMMS and EAM implementation mistakes become evident when you attempt to use collected data for reliability purposes, and that attempt to use it reveals where greater value can be extracted from your systems with careful reconfiguration and process redesign.

Reliability and simulation modeling are computer-based techniques that engineers use to model, mathematically, the behavior of installed systems. They can reveal the location of process bottlenecks and predict whether (and where) another bottleneck is likely to surface once the first is handled. These models can also show the effect of various reliability improvements at different points in the systems and help focus engineering efforts more effectively. In cases where other reliability improvement efforts are failing to deliver expected or desired performance it makes sense to look at process / system design but keep in mind that the results are likely to point in the direction of design changes that could be costly.

The higher reliability achieved through using effective maintenance tactics, will result in less downtime resulting in higher output and higher revenue, and at the lowest cost and lowest risk, including regulatory risks.

Implementation

If you've skipped ahead to this chapter, then you are interested in getting results quickly. Perhaps you are new in your role and you need to turn things around fast. In your role as production manager, general manager, or executive you really don't need to know the details of how to do it. However, you do need the right people doing the right things, and you need to know that Uptime requires your commitment and active leadership.

The Uptime model describes effective practices that are proven to achieve good and even superior results if fully applied. It requires thoughtful and deliberate implementation and cannot just happen on its own. The model comprises 10 components, each of which contributes to the whole result, yet tackling them individually, or only a subset of them, will result in only minimal improvement. ***Don't cherry pick!***

Implementation needs a concerted effort using the entire model in a deliberate and thoughtful manner. It is this awareness that many miss. Knowing this paves the way for going from fair to good to great. The sequencing of your effort, where you begin, and how far you go with each element must be carefully thought through. Overall, the effort requires active executive sponsorship, not just good intentions. Keep in mind that your current state is a result of actions, and perhaps inaction, over a long period of time. That was a result of thinking, beliefs and even emotions within the workforce and its management. There will likely be resistance to change because the future and any change to attain it, can be fearful when letting go of past ways. It will require a full time leader and most likely some outside support. It is an investment in the most important assets you have – your people, thinking and actions, and your business processes.

If you have battled with chronic underperformance from your physical assets, and if maintenance is thought to be at the heart of it, then your challenges could go beyond the obvious process, practice and technical changes that are needed. Leadership (management) may be emotionally tied to the current ways and culture. In some cases, even the identity of key personnel and their self-worth is tied to their work. They can be extremely difficult to help if they haven't admitted to themselves that they might need it.

The journey of excellence in Maintenance Management requires that you implement Uptime reasonably well. The practices and methods are effective if used properly. Each, on its own, is less effective than when combined with the others. The foundation is leadership that you must provide. That entails having a clear vision and direction, plans of action, and the right people doing the right things. You will need to be doing the Essentials reasonably well (not perfectly) before you will really have a chance to target high reliability using the reliability methods. You will have greater success with RCM and PM Optimization if you have a high degree of success in getting your proactive work done on schedule. The results of those analyses often require effective planning, scheduling and schedule compliance to be fully effective.

To achieve that schedule success you need good planning and the right materials to be available when needed. The more proactive work in your maintenance program, the more easily that material supply can be managed. It is far easier to forecast regularly scheduled work, and repairs that are found to be needed before the equipment fails, and hence the materials for them if your work is largely proactive. For the reactive (repair) work that will inevitably still arise, you need risk based algorithms to determine spares requirements, particularly if lead times are long, the components you will need to replace are critical to machine operation and expensive. It's unlikely you will be managing successfully without some degree of measurement of KPIs backed by data gathered and stored in your CMMS. Your existing CMMS may be well configured to help you, but if not, then it too will require effort to extract the value it was originally intended to deliver. Tightening it all up with good documentation, consistency and accuracy of your asset information is needed for compliance to the new global standards in Asset Management.

Implementing Uptime is a project that is aimed at putting a sustainable program of excellence (effective practices) in place. Implementation requires vision and plans based on improvement ideas that are most effective if they come from within your own organization after they know what "good looks like". We use education and training to show our customers what "good looks like". During the training we gather ideas that arise from the class. Those ideas are grouped by theme, improvement projects related to the themes are defined, priorities set, and detailed plans for implementation produced. We do all of that within the classroom environment in a short time when compared with the time it takes to perform a detailed assessment, and in our experience it works just as well, arguably better.

Reliability and maintenance require interactions and inputs from many functional areas in your organization. Your implementation will be at risk if carried out in isolation from those other functional areas within the company. Operations, finance, materials management, human resources and others must be active participants and party to governance of the initiative. Your activities will touch on their areas and they, in turn, will impact on you. We have seen many maintenance improvement initiatives fail because they were conceived and implemented as "maintenance only" or "reliability only".

Good program management governance will keep your initiative on track and avoid the problems that can arise if you are unfocused and have too many initiatives on the go at the same time. It's common to have several disparate initiatives in progress, often with similar goals and competing for the same limited manpower resources.

Your maintenance improvement action items can each be treated as a small project within the broader operational excellence context. Each can have its own action team and leadership. Put as much of the work in the hands of your own people as practical, but be sure to support them with training and needed external help. They are good at doing what you hired them for – such as producing and maintaining. They are not used to implementing major improvement projects and they will need help, training, coaching and possibly other support. They may also need help to simply keep their eye on the ball – it's far too easy to get distracted by the "day-to-day" required by their "real jobs".

Leading change and managing the activities that facilitate a smooth transition will be important. We find it most successful if we don't treat "change management" it as a separate project or work-stream. Do not entrust it to human resources or corporate communications, but engage them in the team leading the transition – they do have valuable roles. Embed transitioning in all that you do and all that you say. As a rule, what we find is the most senior management (executives) and your shop floor people will buy into Uptime quickly. Executives have a mandate to lead change and have a mandate to realize the business case results. The shop floor usually benefits directly in their working life – less instability and chaos, more targeted training and skills enhancement, more time to do the job right instead of doing it over, more work scope as contracted work is brought in house, etc.

Middle management however, it another story. In our experience, this is where you will most likely encounter the greatest resistance and it will be the least obvious. They have a mandate to keep things stable and meet goals that are set in budgets. They may have bonus tied to the status quo and therefore they may feel that their income is threatened by the proposed changes. Remember that managers keep the boat steady and this effort will rock it, sometimes quite a lot.

If they have led efforts to improve performance in the past and not achieved the desired outcomes, they may actually believe that the transition is impossible. They may (and often are) fearful that they will be seen as incompetent for not having made the changes sooner. They may feel guilty about that and they may be trying to hide their own failures. Their happy, enthusiastic and supportive demeanor may be masking a covert effort to sustain the status quo and torpedo the change. Furthermore, they may not even realize they are doing it. They often need help, and for certain their behavior will need to be recognized and dealt with. They must be helped through the transition.

Finally, don't forget that you will need ongoing performance management, audit and senior management reviews to ensure you keep the whole initiative sustained long after the project to implement Uptime has ended. Your goal is to turn Uptime, the framework, into your way of doing things complete with a culture of relentless continuous improvement. It begins with a good project charter, signed and actively supported by top executives and describing how the transition and ongoing programs will be managed. It must be led by a full time dedicated leader, not just treated as a part time initiative. It can deliver seriously great results, so you'll want to treat it like one of your most critical investments, because it will be.

Your Business Case for Change

Initiating your Uptime program requires executive support and some investment. That investment, can pay for itself quite quickly and even be completely self-funding through improvement gains within the first year. That's more than a 100% ROI and it's probably one of your better investments.

Of course you must be willing to grab the value as you make the improvements. If you make that serious and sustained effort to execute correctly and thoroughly you will reduce your costs per unit output and in many cases, quite substantially. It will be worth investing in this, but before you start you'll probably need to get funding. That usually requires a sense of what the program can be worth to your business and what it can cost.

Managing the problem with low reliability in an operational environment is fairly complex. It requires a combination of good maintenance planning and forecasting, good work identification using reliability methods (RCFA and RCM), a combination of standard stores algorithms, sophisticated risk based computational methods, and skilled work execution. Most practitioners in our field specialize in one of those areas and need quite a bit of experience before seeing how the concepts work together to form a beneficial whole. In fact practitioners are almost always technical people with little business education. They don't speak the language of finance and consequently, most practitioners struggle with explaining and putting value to the activities. We've seen a lot of money left on the table by technical people who have failed to get their message of the potential benefits across to the financial decision makers. Reluctance on their part to get help with that has derailed their initiative before it even gets started. Another challenge is that they tend to be quite conservative – they'd rather under-promise and over-deliver, so they understate the potential benefits. Even where they've been able to article a business case, they understate it to the point where it becomes a marginal investment. Of course that does keep them off the hook for producing improved results – not exactly what you want for the business.

By not investing a bit to get professional help, you could be missing a huge payback. As a decision maker who is not in a technical role, you'll need to be watchful for this and perhaps even engage that help even if your technical people insist they don't need it.

Now let's say we now know where value arises. How much can we expect in terms of benefits and where will it show up in our case?

Each organization, industry, location and staff are unique. Market conditions may be different or you may have constraints that others do not have. Consequently, what works well in one operation may or may not work well in yours. Likewise, your willingness to change, to adopt effective practices, restructure if needed, hire, fire, etc. may have an impact on what you can achieve. In quantifying the cost savings and potential we use your data to help determine where you are today.

We apply benchmarks and rules of thumb if needed, to help in determining what might be achievable, and those need to be tempered to match what is doable at your site(s). Each case is unique. How we do that is not presented here. It is too easy to make mistakes if you are doing it for the first time and we'd rather help you get it right.

Your own staff may be able to determine where you are today very well. They may have access to and be good at manipulating your own data, but they may not have access to the sort of benchmarks that are needed to reveal what you could achieve. If they do, then you may be able to determine the potential upside, however, what will it cost to achieve it and how long will it take?

We have seen a number of cases where the customer was able to justify improvement actions, failed to take account of the paybacks and where they will show up, and then under-budget for the help they would need. Consulting rates for good consultants are not at all like what you pay for your own employees and there is a tendency to underestimate costs, then wait for a budget cycle to get the money approved. That really makes no sense though, if you really can get the payback to start early and exceed those costs even in the first year. That is usually doable, so normal accounting and budgeting practices will get in your way. You will need senior finance leaders who can see the interplay of cash flows in and out of different parts of the organization (as opposed to single budget holders who don't see that) to truly grasp the benefit and give approval. If they are good at what they do, they'll see that waiting for a budget cycle actually delays payback and reduces profitability.

Your staff are expert at producing what you sell and maintaining your equipment and systems. They probably have limited exposure to the effective practices as used elsewhere, and very little to no experience in leading a complex transition program. Technical people are often lacking in the sensitivity (emotional intelligence) to effectively deal with the human elements that will invariably arise, even in very technically oriented projects. They are often also lacking in a solid financial business education. They are more likely to be engineers than MBAs or Commerce graduates. They don't speak the language of money and business as well as others in finance and business roles can do.

They will need help to articulate a business case, determine how long the changes will take, how to make them work and more importantly, how to make them stick. You'll need help in estimating the costs of all that effort, and to show the return on investment. Get that help, and the sooner the better in most organizations. If you are even reading this, there's a good chance that Maintenance in your organization, is already failing to deliver the reliability that your assets are capable of achieving. It is likely that to some degree it is already mired in inefficiency, traditional practices, a victim of poor integration between planning and MRO materials, addicted to overtime and the adrenalin rush of being the hero when something breaks. If any of that seems familiar, then you need some help.

Financing

Once you have a solid business case and a plan for implementation to get the returns, you will need to finance the transition. In most cases, if the level of maturity of your maintenance practices is not already high, then the payback from reliability and maintenance improvements will be big. Such initiatives can easily pay for themselves in the first year, but usually not through cost savings. Those will usually come later, but your cost per unit of output can likely be reduced soon. The initial payback is usually through gains in revenues and margin due to improved reliability. The money usually shows up first in revenues, not as an immediate reduction in O&M budgets. Bringing work in-house from contractors, reducing overtime and gains in workforce wrench time will gradually produce cost reductions also.

The "no brainer" opportunity

Let's say that you run your own business. You have an opportunity to invest some money and get a payback that is more than your total investment within the first year. In that case the payback is more than 100% in the first year. Moreover, that payback will continue for many years. Would you invest?

Most entrepreneurs running their own businesses would say yes. After all, the proposition is a "no brainer". Interest earned on putting money into bonds and corporate paper are far less than that. Unless you get really lucky at picking stocks, even a big win on the stock market won't usually give you that great a return. In truth, there aren't a lot of investments with such huge paybacks. Yet many managers in larger companies (which can generally afford the effort quite easily) won't go for it. Why?

What's wrong with those managers?

The quick answer is, nothing really, but you might still wonder why the manager wouldn't go for it. Many managers won't do it simply because it's not their job or the decision needed to approve it are "above their pay grade", so to speak. They may be afraid that they don't have budget to pay for it and they don't have responsibility over the other areas where money will need to be spent (e.g.: training or spare parts) and where the benefits will be realized (revenues). You really need to be a general manager or above to have enough authority to give the green light. Even they may be a bit cautious though because they are not used to working outside the normal budget cycle and process.

Let's assume that we can remove the budget constraint. Would that have an impact on the manager's answer? Sadly, in many cases it does not. Again, it comes back to the difference between management and leadership. The manager's role is to keep things steady and predictable, to follow processes and ensure established practices are used. They are not supposed to shake things up – quite the contrary. That is what leadership does. Again, it comes back to the difference between management and leadership. They are tasked with being risk averse. Many managers won't go for the obvious "no brainer" investment, even if they are not constrained by budget. It is simply not their job – they have a mandate to manage, not to lead. Leaders are sadly often lacking too. Leadership is a personal attribute more than a job description. That's probably why so few managers become senior executives who have a mandate to lead.

If you are in reliability, maintenance or engineering, you are probably a technical person. If you are in operations, you may have a technical background and you may have some business education. However, operational people, like technical people, often lack a deep education in finance and business. It's the finance people who will really appreciate that there are many ways to provide financing for an improvement initiative and they don't all require that you provide budget for them in the maintenance or production / operational department. They need to read this next part!

Financing options

Any project needs investment. That money must come from somewhere and usually that comes in the form of earnings that the project generates. Uptime is no different. When a company wants new physical assets, they will have something tangible that can be sold off if necessary, and it can be used as collateral. Financing in the form of leases, loans, or taking money out of free cash flow are all options. Usually those assets are treated as capital and gradually depreciated over a period of time, but if leased, the cash outlay is treated as an expense and provides more favorable tax treatment.

Improvement initiatives can also be capitalized or treated as expenses – often the latter, and the money is shown in budgets, usually those controlled by those who must do the work (reliability, maintenance and operational departments). The payback however, is seldom reflected in budgets – managers don't usually want to give up budget, even if there are savings, and revenues don't usually show up as offsets to their budgets. If the manager fails to put enough into his budget for the improvement effort, or if the budget for it is not approved, all too often then the initiative slows, stalls or stops. The opportunity to get that great payback is lost. It should not be that way.

Confidence and silos

Of course many managers may lack the needed confidence that they can indeed make the initiative work. They may put money in their budgets for the improvements, but they won't take it back out somewhere else where they expect to see the payback. They may also understate the benefits and focus only on cost savings which will typically show up later rather than sooner.

As is often the case, the investment is required in maintenance, yet the payback is in revenues (not part of any maintenance budget), then there's another barrier – organizational silos. There's a good chance that the budget item won't be approved because there's no obvious payback in the form of short term cost savings in maintenance. That few is far too narrow, but the managers don't have sufficient authority to get past it. The payback shows up as revenues in another silo and budgeting is always done in silos. This holds many initiatives back!

As described already, most reliability and maintenance improvement initiatives do not provide their quickest payback in maintenance savings. The quickest payback is probably going to happen in production (higher production levels) and therefore show up as revenues. Maintenance savings usually take a long time to show up because there's just so much that has to be done before you can take advantage of the increased efficiencies and effectiveness of the reliability program. Reduce the obvious costs too early (labor and materials) and you will probably kill the initiative momentum and potentially drive even greater inefficiencies.

A general manager may have the authority to make the initiative happen. Often, general managers have operational backgrounds and really don't understand the finance nuances as well as you might expect. If they did, then we'd probably see far more improvement initiatives happening.

We really need to engage finance

Financial executives and managers have the right sort of business education and their role usually comes with sufficient authority to get past the accounting, budget and other silo barriers. They are tasked with a broad mandate, making sure that money is spent wisely and in areas where it will provide the highest value. They understand payback and they typically have responsibility for the financial big picture. If they need to spend in area A to get payback in area B, then they can do it. The managers in areas A and B are stuck with only their part of the picture and their budgets. Often, they don't even get to see the big picture, let alone make big picture decisions.

Let's make an offer to your CFO or EVP of finance.

Here's a $20 million dollar project that will pay for itself in the first year and keep paying back at levels exceeding $20 million per year well into the foreseeable future. Like the entrepreneur, your VP Finance or CFO can see the obvious benefit, but he'll still wonder where he's going to find the $20 million. Assuming that he has confidence in your ability to pull it off, then if he had the money, he'd probably say "yes" and go for the gold – he'd be crazy and even fail in his fiduciary duty, if he does not.

But that money wasn't in any budget (those thoughts do still cross his mind) so where will he get it for up-front costs incurred before the payback is realized?

Now we offer him outside financing that does not require payments before the payback starts to come in, and then keeps those payments below the level of benefits that are being realized. The initial $20 million investment is treated like a line of credit (LOC). As the costs of the initiative accrue, the balance of the LOC increases – that money is being used to pay the required outside resources for the initiative. If the payback is expected to start in month 6 for instance, then the first payment against the LOC is at the end of month 6. The amount of the payment can be set below the amount of payback so that the initiative is effectively now paying for itself. That payment continues until the LOC is paid off, however long that takes. Paying it off may take longer than the time it takes to make the improvements and it can always be paid off early. The project remains cash positive for the whole project and the payback continues long beyond it.

What's not to like about that. You get a big payback that covers investment in the first year and you get the money to pay all up-front costs until the project is generating a positive cash flow to pay for itself. Financial people will see that as a good deal and it is possible to set that up if the company has sufficiently good credit to allow for the LOC.

Call to action

Reliability and maintenance improvement projects, if well thought out and crafted, can provide amazingly high returns on investment that would be attractive to any investor. They can be quite easy to finance if the business case is sufficiently well put together and stated. It's important to have the confidence that you can pull it off, and if your maintenance and reliability personnel have been tolerating low performance, then that confidence may be justifiably low. They need help.

If you believe you have a big opportunity, then you probably do. The cost saving and revenue generation opportunities that can be realized through improved asset reliability and more efficient maintenance are fairly easy to spot. Under-performance shows up as high costs, low availability, disappointing production levels, lots of equipment failures and often even as poor plant housekeeping. You don't need help to spot the symptoms.

As a technical or operations manager, you probably need some help to quantify the benefits and scope the improvement initiative. That is best provided by specialists in this larger scale improvement initiatives. The initial investment in doing that sort of up front analysis is not very high and probably something you could, if you have to, even hide in your budget!

Conclusion

This book is intended to help the general manager, the executive in operations and finance, and other non-technical managers to understand what you can and should expect from your reliability and maintenance department. It may also help those reliability and maintenance managers who want to get more from the technology and methods they use. Here the focus has been on the business, not the details.

Good maintenance managers should know this stuff and as a production or general manager, you could now quiz them on it. If you find that they don't know this, then maybe they need help and maybe they don't even know it yet. After all, none of us knows what he or she doesn't know. Hopefully this will open a few eyes.

When John Dixon Campbell wrote the first edition of Uptime (1995) it was intended for operational managers so they could understand the maintenance function better. He himself had a strong operational background and knew that maintenance was often underperforming, and that most managers didn't really know what to do about it. Sadly, only a few of those operational managers bought and read "Uptime", but the maintenance managers did. The feedback John received was that they really liked it because it was the first good and easy to grasp description of what they should be doing that they'd ever seen. However, they wanted more depth and detail, so they got it.

The second and third editions of "Uptime" in 2006 and 2015 respectively, provided that. There's lots of "how to" information out there and yet the situation in many organizations is no different now than it was 24 years ago when Uptime first appeared.

Despite all the information, books, conferences and even videos online, many companies still fail in the area of reliability and maintenance. What's holding them back?

Some are just too comfortable with the status quo and without any external impetus to change, they just chug along and do nothing differently. With what you've learned here you, the general manager, the finance or operations executive can probably provide some external stimulus and spark action.

Keep in mind that many maintenance managers have come up from the tools and probably haven't been exposed to a lot of the information that is available. If they are not all that inclined to be readers, then they may not be fully aware of what's out there. If they are close to retirement, then maybe they don't care anymore either, but you can work on their successors.

There is no shortage of information or advice, but I do believe that a lot of the advice and information is being missed, misapplied or misused. Technical people are natural problem solvers. They like to believe they can figure it out for themselves and solve the problems. Indeed they can do some of it on their own so long as it fits in their specific area of knowledge. I've seen many cases where the technical people have read the books and tried to implement the changes on their own and experienced only partial success. This is particularly the case with engineers in those leadership roles.

The books rarely contain all the information, because so much of it is experiential. The books rarely tell you the tricks and tips needed to make it all work. You might find the odd bit of advice on YouTube or in blogs, but you will spend a lot of time searching and you do need to take what find online with a bit of caution – not all of it is valid nor relevant to your situation.

Technical people (especially engineers) often fail at the human aspects of change. They may have a well-defined and thoroughly planned technical implementation that completely misses the human element. It's as if they follow the Nike slogan of "Just Do It", but few who are around them are likely to "just do it". Even if they've considered the human element of change, the conventional methods so often employed have not always been successful. The result is that, more often than not, they achieve only a partial or failed implementation. Keeping scope of change limited to a responsible "department" is a mistake. Change attempted within a single department alone, won't be very evident to anyone else, even if those other groups are needed to achieve the desired results. For instance, the best planning and scheduling processes will fail if implemented solely within maintenance. If there's inadequacy in MRO materials processes, a lack of integration of those processes with planning and a computer system that cannot be relied upon, the changes won't get you very far.

Failure gets blamed on the methodology or some other external factor. Having pointed a finger elsewhere, the leaders of the initiative may feel justified in walking away from it. They give up and often too easily. As managers, so long as they keep things running reasonably well, there is unlikely to be a lot of pressure to improve. In fact, the failure becomes a reason for not even making another (altered) attempt. Until now.

Once you have read this, as a good production or general managers you are now armed to lead or at least encourage change. Before this, you possibly didn't know enough about this subject to feel comfortable applying pressure. Now that you've read this, you can provide that pressure. As one excellent change leader is James Gowans – he wrote the Foreword to this book. For years, even though he may not have realized it, I've seen Jim as a mentor. When it comes to change he has an excellent perspective, "change requires the relentless application of gentle pressure."

Failures along the way will occur and they should lead to learning and adopting of revised approaches. No single formula will work and we all need to keep learning. If we don't try something new, we won't risk making new mistakes, but we won't change and we won't learn.

As a consultant who has seen many operations in many industries, there are a few common threads I'd like to point out.

One lesson is that if you think you need outside help, then you most probably do. Go with your gut feel on that one. Your displeasure with performance is more than likely warranted and valid. If that under-performance has persisted for any length of time beyond a few months, then it's chronic and requires new eyes and approaches to be improved.

If you already know that performance is below expectations, then you probably don't need an assessment. You already know performance isn't what it should be. Assessments can really help quantify how badly you are doing and what can be done about it, however, they rarely help very much. You do need to define the opportunities, the benefits and the costs to produce a business case, but when this is done in the form of an assessment you will usually alienate those who will ultimately need to change. What's needed is a vision of "what good looks like" (which comes from benchmarking visits and/or training), facilitated reflection on what you are doing in comparison to that vision, ideas from your people (they'll always have many) and then action.

Whenever I am asked by operational or general management to have a look at their sustained poor level of maintenance performance, then I can usually make fairly accurate forecast of what I'll find. Maintenance leadership is probably overworked, under-informed, stuck in their old ways, and/or lacking in motivation to change. Those managers often resist help and outside opinions. Also, and more importantly, they are often a part of the problem. They'll need to admit that to themselves before they'll change, or they'll need to be replaced.

If the maintenance manager is relatively new, then he could be struggling with just how to get started and most often those managers welcome some outside help. Nothing in the career path of most reliability and maintenance managers ever prepares them to lead change initiatives and their usually strong technical background doesn't prepare them to look at business as a business, nor at the complex world of human factors that will conspire to resist any change. He or she may be reluctant to ask for help, but they are often open to it. Chances for success are high, provided they don't try to do it all themselves.

Maintenance managers who call for help with being forced to do so, are usually new to the role or to their company. They see the mess, know that much must be done, but lacking a lot of extra resources (and usually battling with a lot of emergencies), they just can't get started and sustain it. Fortunately, because they are new they don't feel responsible for having created or tolerating the mess, so they don't mind asking for help nor seeing it change for the better.

As a general manager, operational or production manager, or executive you can easily discern which situation you have. Your support, encouragement and help to the maintenance manager is probably needed and in the right cases, welcomed. Start now.

Lightning Source UK Ltd.
Milton Keynes UK
UKHW050309081121
393541UK00001B/2